ADVANCE PRAISE

"This is a story of a young girl coming of age in a frightening and dangerous world. It's a story of determination and hope and of holding on to your own humanity while overcoming adversity, both political and personal. Suzette Sheft chronicles her grandmother's escape from Nazi Austria with empathy and care and tells the story without embellishment or over-sentimentality. In an era fraught with antisemitism and Holocaust denial, *Running for Shelter* is an important contribution that sheds light on the diversity of experience in the Holocaust. It is also a work of love and a testament to the depth of Sheft's connection to her family story." **—Dana Raucher, Executive Director of The Samuel Bronfman Foundation and Board Member of the Jewish Book Council**

"Beautifully crafted, carefully researched, and altogether from the heart. In sharing the story of her grandmother's journey through the Holocaust, Suzette Sheft has emerged as an important new voice in the transmission of memory from generation to generation." — **Rabbi Elliot Cosgrove, Park Avenue Synagogue, Manhattan**

"It is now more important than ever that we listen to, and learn from, Holocaust survivors. We must remember their stories and take time to remember those who are not able to speak for themselves. Reading the story of a survivor offers a unique opportunity to take a small and simple action, and at the same time, be part of something bigger and very meaningful. I'm grateful to Suzette for writing and sharing her incredible grandmother's story in this vital and impactful book."— **Dov Forman, author of the New York Times bestseller *Lily's Promise***

"Suzette Sheft not only deserves praise for her mature and evocative telling of her grandmother's story, but for her commitment to telling it. At USC Shoah Foundation, we are honored to be caretakers of Suzette's grandmother, Monique (Inge) Sheft's recorded testimony. We can't do it alone—Suzette's generation also holds this responsibility, and this book is a beautiful embodiment of this duty. Thank you, Suzette, for your commitment to your grandmother's legacy. As a result, you protect the legacy of the Holocaust, and every survivor." —**Kori Street, Finci-Viterbi, Interim Executive Director, USC Shoah Foundation**

RUNNING FOR SHELTER

A TRUE STORY

HOLOCAUST BOOKS FOR YOUNG ADULTS

SUZETTE SHEFT

ISBN 9789493276680 (ebook)

ISBN 9789493276505 (paperback)

ISBN 9789493276512 (hardcover)

Publisher: Amsterdam Publishers, The Netherlands

info@amsterdampublishers.com

Running for Shelter is part of the series Holocaust Books for Young Adults

Cover art: Girl running by Rekha Arcangel (Arcangel) and airplane spot art by Stephen Mulcahey (Arcangel)

Cover design: Iain Barr

Author photograph: Brian Marcus

CONTENTS

AUTHOR'S NOTE

When I was 13, I watched my father die after losing a two-year battle with pancreatic cancer. Despite the years of suffering, his death still felt incredibly sudden, and without his unmatched sense of joy, love, and knowledge, the world felt unfamiliar. When he was alive, he would tell me stories about his life while tucking me in each night, but in the months following his death, I could only try to connect the foggy and mismatched puzzle pieces of his recollections. I fantasized about rewinding time, so I could go back and record my favorite stories about his childhood. Instead, I had to replay disjointed versions of them in my mind. I wished I had taken the time to write these stories down when I had the chance, because his death allowed me to understand the vitality of preserving the stories of our loved ones before it is too late. I knew I could not let my father's story—or any other story, for that matter—fade away.

As I write this author's note, I am 15 years old and living in New York City. I began writing this book when I was 13 in order to preserve and share the unique experience of my grandmother, Inge Eisinger—now Monique Sheft—who lived through the Holocaust.

For as long as I can remember, I have been fascinated by reading about the Holocaust and World War II and visiting the Holocaust museums with my father in almost every city we traveled to, because of my Omi's stories as a survivor. But it was not until I read her first-person, three-page account of her escape from Austria that I truly understood how impactful her story was to me. At that moment, I knew I wanted to combine my desire to write with my passion of learning about the Holocaust and my family members' stories, so I decided to record Omi's World War II journey in the form of a novel. My father greatly encouraged me on this path when I discussed the book idea with him.

Although it may be too late to record the stories of ancient genocides with no living survivors, it is not too late to record those of the Holocaust—so I set out to do just that. Over multiple days, I interviewed my grandmother about her escape from Vienna, Austria, to Buxières-les-Mines, France. I also watched an interview conducted by the USC Shoah Foundation about her story to widen my perspective. I took extensive notes, and subsequently, the process of writing, re-writing, and editing my manuscript commenced. This project has allowed me to share the voices of those who have, for so long, been oppressed.

Although my father was alive when I started writing this book, he passed away before I finished the manuscript. His death prompted me to realize the importance of giving a voice to those silenced through writing, before it is too late—just as it was with him. I would give anything for my dad to read this book.

In loving memory of Dad,

Thank you for believing in,
supporting, and inspiring me.

I love you.

1 MAY 22ND, 1937

VIENNA, AUSTRIA

"O dear Augustin, Augustin, Augustin..."

Inge could hear joyous singing coming from the kitchen. The sugary smell of strawberries, apricots, and raspberries wafted through the gold-adorned living room, down the painting-lined hallway, and up into Inge's nose. A wide, toothy grin nestled in between her rosy cheeks, and her stomach rumbled loudly. Jam season had begun in the Eisinger household!

Inge flew out of her room, her pale pink flats smacking against the hardwood floor. Her mother's sculptures, perched on the shelves above, seemed to watch her as though acting as a second pair of eyes for Stella.

The hallway brought Inge to the formal living room, one of her mother's favorite places to entertain. The white walls were decorated in gold trimming, and chic white couches formed a large entertaining area. An elaborate chandelier hung from the ceiling, crystals dripping from its golden arms.

Inge cautiously made her way through the grand room, careful not to leave a spot of dirt on the cream rug, and finally arrived at her destination. The kitchen was a forbidden zone for her, and Inge glanced anxiously behind her with wide green eyes and then, gigging with excitement, pushed open the swinging doors and skipped into the bright, spacious kitchen.

Inside, the scene was chaotic, but still resembled something out of a fairy tale. A dozen women dressed in uniforms of white aprons, gloves, and short-sleeved gray dresses circled the marble island in the center of the room. Each woman wore her hair pulled back in a tight bun.

Inge plopped down onto a nearby chair at the whitewashed kitchen table where the family's chef Marcel often sneaked Inge's favorite snack, pork fat, to her. The earthy aromas of fruit tickled her nose, and the songs of the women perked up her ears. She immediately recognized the soothing voice of their maid, Clara, standing out above the others. The rest of the women's voices created a comforting harmony.

They began to sing a song by Camilla Frydan, one of Inge's favorite singers. Inge jumped off the chair to dance, her white dress blossoming around her like the petals of a lily. Her red curls bounced off her shoulders, and her face flushed with color. At that moment, all of her worries drifted away.

"May I please help you with the jam?" Inge asked once the song was over.

The women did not answer.

Grabbing the top edge of the island, Inge pulled herself up so that they could see her and asked again, louder, "I don't mean to be a pest, but I was wondering if I could assist you with making the jam? I could be the taste tester!" She licked her lips, imagining the sea of red, purple, and orange goodness filling her mouth.

The women ignored her still and began singing again—even Clara, who so often talked and joked with Inge.

The staff of the household usually responded to her promptly, so she raised her voice, "Excuse me, may I please help? I love jam, and I have always wanted to learn how to make it!"

Finally, Clara stopped and answered, "Inge, we would love your help, but we have strict instructions from your mother. So you'll have to ask Ms. Stella first."

Inge flashed an appreciative smile, which quickly vanished as she considered asking her mother for permission. Surely Stella would decline Inge's request. Before she could figure out how to proceed, the white door swung open, and Stella charged into the kitchen.

Her permed brown hair complemented her polished face and bright brown eyes. Thin pearl necklaces were stacked neatly over the bodice of her crisp black dress, perfectly coordinating with her cream heels, which clacked against the wood floor as she paced around the kitchen. Inge thought that her mother looked like a movie star.

"Why has the singing stopped?"

"It was my fault, Mutti. They were just answering my question," Inge mumbled, staring at the ground, always afraid of upsetting her mother. "I asked if I could help them make the jam, and maybe taste it."

"Inge, I cannot believe that despite being eight years old, you still manage to forget the rules!" scolded Stella in a harsh tone. She bent down to her daughter's level. "First of all, you do *not* need any more sugar, and you aren't even supposed to enter the kitchen without permission. Secondly, the workers are not permitted to stop singing when making jam, so I know they are not eating the fruit. You know there aren't many others in Vienna with the same access to this wonderful fresh fruit supply. Let them work! And Clara, you should know better than to stop singing during jam season! I am very disappointed in you." She turned back to her daughter. "We will talk about your punishment later. Now, out!" she directed, pointing toward the door.

Inge walked out of the room ahead of her mother, sulking. "I am sorry for disrespecting your wishes, Mutti," she said.

"Good heavens, Inge," Stella went on. "How many times must I tell you to remain in your room when the women are here working? You are not to disrupt their progress!"

Inge knew better than to roll her eyes, but she did it inwardly. As

Stella never explained anything to her daughter, Inge thought it was very hypocritical of her mother to say that she should know better.

"I will just go back to apologize to Clara," Inge said softly.

"Quickly!" Stella huffed, and Inge reentered the kitchen.

"I'm very sorry for disrupting your work and causing this commotion," Inge announced to the women sincerely. But she had really returned for the canister of powdered sugar that sat on the counter. She grabbed it and darted back out again.

Back in her room, she quietly opened her window just high enough for her arm to fit through. She covered the outside of the windowpane with the sugar, and then drew a heart so large that it took up her whole window. As a final touch, she added her name at the bottom of the heart.

Delighted, Inge pulled her arm back in and admired her work. With a signal this large, the stork would surely notice the sugar on her window and finally bring her a baby sibling.

Inge pranced across her room to the opposite window and gazed into the elegant neighborhood below. Orchid petals drifted down onto the street, where prominent Viennese families were making their way to St. Stephen's Cathedral for ceremonial mass. A sleek emerald automobile gracefully roamed the avenue, as if observing the scene through its white headlights. Flowers blossomed around the Gothic cathedral.

Inge's eyes followed a young couple practically floating down the sidewalk. The man wore an ash-colored suit while the woman's delicate pink dress, thin gold necklace, and lavish hat reminded Inge of her mother's everyday outfits. *Were they in love?* she wondered. They certainly looked happy with each other.

Shifting her gaze to the towers of the cathedral, Inge noticed that they were decorated for the special event. The south tower—Stella called it "*Steffl*"—boasted a row of candles along its top turret, while the north tower's black iron bell produced lively rings throughout Vienna. After the 11th ring, the few remaining people on the sidewalk rushed up the cathedral steps and slipped in between its slowly closing wooden doors.

Of all the exciting things to see outside her window, Inge most enjoyed looking at the cathedral itself. St. Stephen's, she had learned at school, was built 600 years earlier by King Albert and his sons, and she thought it was one of the most beautiful buildings in the city. The roof was covered by 230,000 glazed mosaic tiles that reflected sunlight into her bedroom each morning, waking her like a natural alarm clock. From her window, she could examine the cathedral's Gothic features and limestone walls up close. In fact, she sometimes shared her secrets with the elaborate statue of the Franciscan friar that stood at the Capistran Chancel. The friar looked purposeful, his arms spread apart in a grand welcome, the Austrian flag proudly waving from his left hand. He was stepping victoriously down upon a rebel Turk, while above him a brilliant golden sunburst shone over protective guardian angels. Sometimes, when Inge was afraid in the darkness of the night, she looked out at him and, believing he would protect her, soon drifted peacefully off to sleep.

Gazing back down at the people walking on the promenade, Inge longed to look like the beautiful, slim women she saw there. She wished her round body looked like theirs and her mother's.

2 NOVEMBER 10TH, 1938 (POST-KRISTALLNACHT)

VIENNA, AUSTRIA

One kilometer from St. Stephen's Cathedral stood a block filled with Jewish-owned stores—all of them glass-filled, dirt-tracked, and looted. The Star of David and the word *Jude* in big black capital letters had been spray-painted on nearly every door.

One elderly man, his salt-and-pepper eyebrows furrowed, inspected the shattered windows of his defaced shoe store, staring at the remains with defeated brown eyes. His sign, "Albert's Shoes and Shine" had once proudly perched above his front entrance. Now it hung limply from one nail like a fallen soldier slain by his persecutors. Not a single piece of inventory remained. The shoeboxes littering the stained hardwood floor were shoeless, the gaping register was empty, and the couches were nothing more than mountains of stuffing. Albert's wife silently swept out their vandalized store, pressing her lips into a tight line as if afraid to even speak.

The store owners winced as they heard boots pounding the paved road, like the beating of a drum. A mob was approaching. The rioters wore oversized poster boards hanging from their necks by long pieces of string. The big, bold lettering read: "*Austrians! Defend yourself! Don't buy from Jewish-owned stores!*" Marching in sync, the Nazis chanted these words in German accents thicker than those of the Austrians. Their angry words shot into the Jewish couple's hearts like bullets. Albert's grieving heart yearned to give up, yet he stood tall in front of his store, proud amidst the remnants of his family's legacy and its memories. The group of Nazis threatened to engulf the elderly Jew, their fiery eyes burning holes into his dignity.

"Shame on you," croaked Albert.

Then, one of the rioters' smirks broke, and he splattered his saliva across Albert's face.

Three blocks from the Jewish stores, Inge waited with her governess Maria in a line circling the corner to buy tickets for the movie *Heidi*. Across the street from the theater stood a row of Christian-owned businesses, white and polished and without a scratch, their storefronts as clean as freshly painted fences.

A light breeze stirred red, orange, and yellow leaves around the sidewalk. To entertain herself, Inge jumped on them, crunching them beneath her boots. As the line moved forward, she amused herself by guessing the names of the workers inside each shop they passed. *Rosemarie, who will soon marry a prince,* she thought, as she spied a young coffee shop waitress.

"How much longer until we can go in?" Inge complained to Maria, dancing around on the sidewalk. They had just inched by a black, question mark-shaped lamp post, which she counted as the fourth they had passed.

"Now, Inge, you must present yourself in a ladylike manner. Would you like your mother to receive a bad report? You know that young ladies do not whine," Maria replied in a firm tone.

"Sorry, *Moiselle,*" she mumbled, using the crude nickname for *mademoiselle* that Maria despised. Maria was always scolding her and threatening to tell Stella, but today Inge didn't care. She was too excited to see *Heidi*.

At last, they were on the same street as the theater, and Inge watched anxiously as each person in front of her bought tickets from the box office attendant. As they finally arrived at the front of the line, the synchronized beat of boots caught her ear, and Inge turned her head toward the street.

A troop of Hitler Youth marched down in single file, singing "*Es zittern die morschen Knochen,*" their official song. The girls in the troop all wore their hair the same way, in two braids with small bows tied at the bottom. Their official black coats were adorned with a red and white armband centered by a black swastika. As the group passed, a few people cheered; others abruptly turned around and walked in the other direction.

The troop began passing out flyers to the moviegoers, and a pretty teenage girl pressed one into Maria's hand before Inge could read its message: "Not one penny to the Jews."

The group's leader, an older German soldier in a shiny black cap, strode up to the woman behind the box office window. Inge felt Maria grasp her arm and pull her sharply away from the man. She noticed her governess settle her gaze on the ground. Inge could sense the uneasiness of everyone around her and wondered who this group was. Unable to see the box office or understand what was going on, she kept her head high and watched as the man beckoned his troop toward the ticket agent.

"My troop gets tickets for half the price," he commanded.

"Of-of course, sir. Let me get those for you now."

Turning, the SS soldier yelled, "Attention!"

All of the troop members formed a single line, raising their right arms in salute.

Inge watched the girls in the group with awe. They looked like the friends she wanted to have, instead of her governess and maid.

"*Moiselle,* I want to be part of this girl scout troop. Look, they get half-price tickets at the movie theater!"

Maria's eyes widened in horror, and her cheeks turned a light shade of red.

When Inge was barely a year old, Stella had divorced her father, Ludwig Eisinger. Only together for two years, the couple's marriage had always been strained. Inge and her father had a very impersonal, distant relationship; they saw each other once a year on Inge's birthday.

One of the main reasons Stella had divorced Ludwig was because their views on religion were contradictory. He was a proud practicing Jew who went to synagogue on every Jewish holiday and almost every Friday night. Stella, on the other hand, was legally a Jew, but she was not proud of being one. She sought to leave Judaism in her past and refused to raise her daughter as a practicing Jew. No one outside of their immediate family even knew that Stella and Inge were Jewish. Even Inge didn't know.

Inge looked at Maria, who hesitantly replied, "I-I think you should talk to your mother about joining." Maria did not think it was her job to explain to Inge what the troop was really all about.

3 NOVEMBER 14TH, 1938

VIENNA, AUSTRIA

Inge rushed through the door of the apartment ahead of Maria and dropped her schoolbooks into a pile on the floor. Then she sank down next to them on the plush Oriental rug and removed her black outdoor flats.

"Inge! It is not at all ladylike to be sitting on the floor in a dress," Maria scolded. "And it is certainly not proper to just throw down your belongings," she went on, snatching up the shoes.

Wanting to escape Maria's glare, Inge ran into the living room to see if Stella was home. She stopped short, frozen in place. The once-embellished and spirited room was now naked. The chic white couches and cocktail tables were gone, exposing barren hardwood floors. Stella's masterful sculptures and paintings were missing. Inge felt like all the glamor in the house had suddenly disappeared. She needed to find her mother and insist that she explain what had happened to their things, but Inge feared the confrontation. She knew that her mother would dismiss her as she always had, refusing to answer questions or offer any solace. Inge decided that an afternoon snack might make her feel better instead.

"Marcel, will you please prepare me a fruit platter with some tea cakes?" she called from the hallway. Then she collapsed onto a dining room chair, inwardly and sarcastically thanking Stella for not giving away all of their furniture. Moments later, the kitchen door swung open, but instead of Marcel or Clara, it was Inge's grandmother Anna who entered. She was carrying a plate of cookies.

"Omi! You never make me cookies!" Inge jumped from the chair and hugged Anna. "Thank you so much for the snack!" she exclaimed, grabbing a warm *Vanillekipferl.*

"You're welcome, my dear. It will be our secret," Anna winked. "Now, let's sit so that you can tell me about your day at school. Did you enjoy it?"

Inge related to her, as she had to Maria on the walk home, how Elias Gruber had pulled her hair during their arithmetic lesson because of its "disgusting" color. Her grandmother nodded and gasped appropriately, sharing her outrage, but Inge could tell that her mind was elsewhere.

"Is everything okay, Omi?" she asked, pausing her story.

"Of course, my love. Tell me what happened next."

A small knot formed in the pit of Inge's stomach. She expected evasive replies from Stella, but her grandmother was normally more open. Inge hesitantly continued her tale—conveniently leaving out the part about stomping on Elias' foot in retaliation—and then decided that she had a right to know what was going on. "Omi, what happened to our furniture, and where are Marcel and Clara?" she asked.

Anna took a long, deep breath. "Inge, Marcel and Clara will not be working here anymore. This will also be Maria's last day with us. You will be home much more than you usually are." Anna paused. "You are going to be homeschooled by me from now on."

Inge's eyes grew large. "I don't have to go to school anymore?" She could not believe her good fortune—she would never have to hear Elias Gruber compare her hair to fire again! Anna would be present in her life each day and Maria would no longer be bossing her around. But Inge realized that she would also miss out on the celebration of St. Leopold's Day and the invitations to her classmates' birthday parties. And Marcel, the chef, would also be gone. This made Inge especially sad. Reflecting on her loss, anger crept in and replaced her sorrow. Why did her mother always send everyone away? Why did she always take everything from her?

Inge decided it was time to find out. She ran from the dining room, leaving a bewildered Anna at the table.

Stella was lounging in her bedroom on her lavish navy sofa when Inge burst in.

"Mutti, what is happening?" she exclaimed in a high wail of alarm.

Stella had known this moment would come eventually, and had vowed to keep her emotions masked to deescalate her daughter's panic. "It's just the way things are now," she flatly replied without looking up from her magazine.

Inge was stunned. She felt as if she had been slapped. How could her mother lie there without a care in the world while their belongings and loyal staff disappeared? She would not even offer an explanation! Inge was reminded of the time when Stella returned home from a trip abroad newly married, bringing a strange man into their home and expecting Inge to accept him. She could not believe that her mother had made such an important decision without even telling her beforehand. Inge felt betrayed, and she had complained about her mother's rash behavior to the only classmate she could call a friend, Grete Bauer. When Grete shared Inge's secret with the other children in their class, they all laughed because they thought it was a joke, and Inge had laughed with them. Shortly after, Stella and her new husband were divorced.

These things were normal for Inge. Her mother was entirely unlike the nurturing, doting mothers of her classmates, and her lifestyle was largely different. Almost every night, she either went out or had friends over at the apartment for dinner parties. Stella never tucked her daughter into bed or kissed her goodnight. Hearing about her classmates' family dinners and trips stabbed Inge with jealousy and longing. Why couldn't her mother be more like them?

A pounding at the apartment door tore Inge from her thoughts.

"Inge, ask Omi to please get the door," Stella commanded with disinterest. "I am going to the kitchen."

Inge instinctively ran to the door herself, an act of defiance to her mother. Turning the knob, she opened it and faced a gaunt, brown-haired man whose oversized ears flanked a creased and discolored bowler. Inge's eyes widened, and her hand fell numbly to her leg. "Papa?" she asked incredulously.

His round face had thinned and aged so significantly since she had last visited with him one year ago that he was nearly unrecognizable.

"Inge, it is me," he said, declining an awkward hug and brusquely pushing past her. "Where is your mother?"

His ambivalence was nothing new for Inge, but she was still stung by it. Almost a year had gone by, and this was his greeting?

Ludwig stalked toward the kitchen and slammed the door shut behind him. A loud gasp penetrated the closed door as a tin pan fell clattering onto the ground. Inge realized that her mother was just as surprised to see him as she was.

Inge tiptoed to the kitchen and pressed her ear against the cool white door.

"I told you not to come here, Ludwig!"

"Stella, you have to let go of our past disagreements and be reasonable. My life is at stake!"

"Ludwig—"

"I lost my job because everyone at work knows who I really am. I have no money, nowhere to turn, and now I am hearing of mass arrests! I am not safe anywhere, especially not in my own home. Let me stay here! Please," cried Ludwig. "They will not be looking for me in your house!"

"Enough, Ludwig! I owe you nothing. You know I cannot let you stay here."

"You used my family and took our money, and this is how you repay us!"

"Ludwig, you would be putting all of our lives in danger. Think of your daughter."

"Stella, you are just as much a danger, even if you pretend you are not—"

Inge was suddenly pried away from the door. Looking up, she saw Anna holding her by the collar and glaring disapprovingly.

"Now, Inge, you know better than to eavesdrop on your parents. Go sit in your room until they have figured this out." Anna rarely spoke to her granddaughter like this, and Inge stormed to her room in disappointment. She left her door open to listen in, however, and noticed that her grandmother lingered in the hallway herself.

Suddenly, with a thundering *whoosh* and a *boom*, the front door of the apartment crashed to the floor.

Anna was the first to reach the entranceway, with Inge trailing close behind.

Three men in gray-green uniforms stood on the threshold of the apartment. A red swath of cloth embroidered with a black *x* shape—its ends bent at right angles—hugged their sleeves. Inge instantly recognized the symbol from the day at the movie theater. Gold and silver pins lined their lapels and crisp caps, and guns were hanging menacingly at their sides.

Inge stared at their smug faces, her wide green eyes meeting their icy glares. The sight of their guns cemented her to the spot. She was unable to move, and she forgot where she was or who she was with. Terrified, she wondered if the men were there to shoot her and her family.

"Line up against the wall, you Jewish rats!" screamed one officer who Inge deemed the leader of the group, judging by his wrinkled face and stained yellow teeth.

One of the younger men cast his bright blue eyes into the older man's stern gaze for approval. Inge recognized his want, for she had cast the same look upon Stella many times.

The older officer nodded.

"Move, or I shoot," yelled the younger one, pointing his gun at Anna.

Inge's legs were leaden, and it took all of her concentration to move them. The harsh voices around her became nothing more than buzzing, and blood roared in her ears.

"Don't worry, Inge."

A shaking voice penetrated her hearing, and a sweaty palm grabbed her cold hand. "I know you're afraid," continued Anna. "I am too, but you have to listen to them, or else these men will get us in trouble."

Inge allowed her grandmother to guide her out of the entryway.

The young guard led them down the hallway to join Ludwig and Stella, who were standing in the bare living room. Inge's stilted pace angered him, so the guard jabbed at her spine with the muzzle of his gun. Her back arched at the feeling of the cold metal.

Once the family was united in the living room, Inge stole a glance at the others: Anna, still clasping her hand, had tears running down her cheeks. Stella stood tall in the room's center, recklessly staring down the younger officer. Ludwig barely stood at all; he was down on one knee, hunched over with his hands clutching his stomach.

"I ordered you to line up against the wall, *now*!" the shortest of the three officers commanded. Anna gently pushed Inge toward the empty wall, then she helped Ludwig rise and allowed him to lean upon her as he hobbled toward his daughter.

Inge could see that her father was unwell. He had taken two blows from the short guard, and now sweat dripped down his pale skin. Ludwig tried to conceal his fear, but his lips quivered and his arms shook.

Stella joined them at the wall and stood as still as one of her statues.

"We were alerted by the concierge that an ugly *Jude* had illegally entered the building," began one of the officers, glaring at Ludwig.

"He recognized you from that filthy synagogue, Stadttempel, across town."

Inge had only heard these terms in passing and did not understand why they would get her Papa in trouble.

"You and your family will soon enjoy a trip to—"

Unexpectedly, Inge's scarf fell from her head, revealing her beautiful locks of red hair.

The men stared, expressionless. The leader directed his eyes into Inge's frightened green ones. She still clutched Anna's hand.

"Why is the *Jude* staying here with you and the child?" he asked Anna, perplexed.

"What do you mean? I live here alone with my daughter and granddaughter!"

Stella suddenly turned to Ludwig. "How dare you come and try to hide here?" she yelled. "We have not seen you in years! Explain yourself!"

The officers became even further incensed by her revelation. "Is this true?" spat the leader, edging his face so close to Ludwig's that they nearly touched.

Looking down at his scuffed brown shoes, Ludwig closed his eyes and nodded imperceptibly.

"You disgust me! Hiding behind women and children like the coward you are!"

The other two men circled Ludwig. He was pushed to the floor, pulled up again, and pinned to the wall. The older man punched him in the stomach, and Inge watched the light leave her father's eyes with each hit. Fear crested in her throat. *Were they going to kill her father? What would they do to her?*

The three men laughed. Gripping Ludwig by the collar and pointing a gun at his back, they escorted him out of the apartment.

"Help me!" choked Ludwig, but his pleas were lost in the stomping of the Nazi boots over the sharp debris of the broken door.

4 NOVEMBER 20TH, 1938
VIENNA, AUSTRIA

November 20th was Inge's favorite day of the year. After nearly a week of remaining in her room for most of the day—leaving only sporadically, for snacks—Inge leaped out of bed early and rushed to her brown armoire, where she put on her finest dress and flats. Looking at herself in the mirror, she knew that her outfit needed a final touch. She rummaged through her hair accessories until she found the missing piece to her outfit: a silver tiara. Placed in the center of her hair, this tiara would remind everyone that today was a special day. Inge was turning nine.

In the kitchen, Stella and Anna greeted her with a thin slice of bread embellished by a sliver of butter.

Inge's face fell as she observed the empty table: there was no extravagant breakfast, flowers, or birthday cards—just an empty, ice-cold room.

"Happy birthday, Inge!" exclaimed Anna, drawing her granddaughter out of her disappointment and into a warm hug.

"Thank you, Omi," Inge responded, pulling away. She was glad that her grandmother had acknowledged her birthday, but she wished more than anything that she could have been greeted with her traditional celebratory breakfast.

"Happy birthday, Inge," whispered Stella. "My nine-year-old is growing up so fast."

Inge could tell that something was wrong with her mother. After the confrontation in their home, Stella's behavior had changed. She stopped grooming her hair into perfect waves, pearl earrings no longer dangled from her ears, and her face was always serious. Furniture continued to disappear, and Stella stopped hosting parties and sculpting in her workshop. She had lost her creative spirit.

"Thank you, Mutti."

Inge excused herself. Her earliest birthday memories were of finishing her special breakfast and rushing to the living room, where she was greeted by cards and presents from family. She prayed that this birthday would be redeemed, but her face fell when she saw that the room was empty. There were no birthday decorations, and she felt forgotten.

Standing in the stark room, Inge thought back to the previous year.

"Happy Birthday, Inge!" shout the excited voices as I walk into the dining room. Little girls line the table, holding neatly wrapped presents that match the silver balloons hanging in the hallway. With my long white gown and a silver tiara on my perfectly curled red hair, I feel like a princess.

The dining room has been transformed from chic white to posh purple for my birthday party. Purple cups coupled with matching straws adorn the oak table, and on top of Mutti's finest china lay cheese and crackers, fruit, and an assortment of meat for my guests to nibble on.

Sitting at the head of the dining room table, the seat usually reserved for Mutti, I take in the whole scene. On either side of the table, my classmates talk in the same quiet, polite tone that Maria has taught me to speak in. While they slowly eat the lunch of pork shank prepared by Marcel, I eat the pork fat that he saved for me. My birthday is the only time Mutti allows me to have this delicacy, even though I eat it without her permission all the time.

This party is perfect, identical to every birthday I have had for as long as I can remember.

"Inge, open my present first," Mutti insists, handing me an oval-shaped gift wrapped in purple paper.

Smiling, I rip off the wrapping and find inside the only present I had asked for: a glass container of creamy, yellow mustard.

Delighted, I quickly unscrew the silver cap and smell the spicy aroma. "Oh!" I exclaim. "Thank you, Mutti! This is the best birthday present ever!"

Mutti laughs as I plunge my spoon into the jar and remove a heaping mouthful.

Special meals, Mutti's most expensive china, and elegant celebrations have all become a part of my birthday tradition. Yet, my favorite aspect of these parties is that the other children clamor for my attention. I crave their friendships because I am usually only accompanied by Mutti's staff.

"This is such a wonderful party, Inge," exclaims Helga, the daughter of one of Mutti's friends. Since Helga is two years older than I am, I do not know her very well; we only spend time together when our mothers arrange it, which is rare.

"You are so sweet," I reply, blushing and noticing Clara clearing away the rest of my guests' plates. My cheeks warm instantly. I know what is coming next.

The guests continue to converse in muted tones, but the chatter is interrupted as Mutti flips the lights off and walks into the dining room holding a double-layer vanilla cake stacked with eight candles on a gold plate.

The children start singing together. Their small faces look bigger in the candlelight, and their voices grow louder.

"Happy birthday to you

Happy birthday to you
Happy birthday, dear Inge..."

Inge shook herself out of her reverie as she heard Anna calling. She felt utterly disappointed. Her birthday wish was for it to be her eighth birthday again.

5 NOVEMBER 27TH, 1938

VIENNA, AUSTRIA

Still groggy from a fitful night's sleep, Inge walked out of her room and into chaos. From the hall, she saw Stella tearing through a closet, throwing clothes into a large suitcase on the bed. From the kitchen, she heard the clatter of silverware and crockery being dumped onto the countertop.

Inge lurked into her mother's room, stepping over piles of expensive shoes and linens, treading carefully so as not to wrinkle anything on the floor. "Mutti, what's going on?" She peeked into the large dressing room and gasped. The shiny pairs of high heels that had once lined the organized shelves were gone, and the glamorous dresses had also vanished. The empty rods were like skeletal bones. The starkness of the closet alarmed Inge, but Stella's disheveled appearance worried her more. "Is everything okay, Mutti?"

"Everything is fine, Inge, but pack a small bag," her mother replied coolly as she continued to sort through her clothes. "We're leaving this afternoon."

"What? But why? Is Omi coming with us?"

"No, Omi doesn't want to travel anywhere right now, so she will be staying here in Vienna for the time being."

Stella's clipped responses left Inge feeling hurt. Flustered, she stomped out of the room. The suddenness of everything overwhelmed her. It had been only two weeks since the furniture started to disappear, she'd stopped attending school, the staff was fired, and three strange men took her father away. Now, out of nowhere, they were leaving Vienna, and her mother would not even tell her why.

Inge walked to her window to look at the magnificent view of St. Stephen's Cathedral. She noticed the faint outline of the heart she had drawn with sugar on the window just a few weeks before and realized that a piece of herself would forever stay in this apartment. She started to daydream, bittersweet memories of her time with Marcel and Clara, when she was interrupted by her mother's shouting.

"Inge, are you ready? We are going to be late if we don't leave now!"

"Coming, Mutti," Inge answered. She grabbed as many clothes as she could and stuffed them into her small bag, hoping they would suit her—wherever she might be going.

Stella led them through the massive glass doors of the spacious train station, bringing a gloved hand to her nose instinctively in the stale air. Stella glanced up at the face of the large marble clock above the competing food vendors and restless ticket tellers. They were late. "We must hurry, Inge!" she called, taking her daughter by the arm.

Carving a path through the mob of businessmen, distressed parents, and whining children, Stella walked while her daughter tripped along behind her. At the entrance to the platform, their progress halted abruptly. Three patrolling guards of the French Third Republic were blocking the doorway that led to the trains.

"Excuse me," Stella said, and the guards eyed her for a few

seconds before stepping aside, revealing a balding ticket clerk at a tidy desk.

Inge pressed closely to her mother. She pretended that they were in a movie with Stella as the star. The film began with them having to cross a border guarded by a wall of soldiers to get to their destination. Stella was the heroine, of course, and she would see them through this danger. To Inge, her mother was as inspiring and beautiful as any movie star she had ever seen.

Stella pulled a yellow envelope from her purse, removing their passports and train tickets. Thrusting the documents at the clerk, she bit her bright red lip in an attempt to mask her unease. Under the air of composure and calm, she prayed that he would not notice the passports were a forgery.

The man squinted over a pair of small square glasses balancing on his nose and flipped through each page of Stella's passport. His pale face was expressionless as his eyes darted back and forth between Stella and her photograph. Nodding, he scribbled something down in a thick ledger.

Stella shifted uncomfortably, but the clerk soon moved on to Inge's credentials, and she felt her worry begin to lift. *Halfway there*, she thought. He examined Inge's picture while Stella held her breath. Her daughter's papers had been hurried; she knew they should have found someone more trustworthy to forge their documents. But suddenly, with a heavy *thud, thud, thud, thud*, the clerk stamped the passports and train tickets, and Stella exhaled.

"Have a lovely trip to Lausanne, ma'am," stated the clerk, handing the documents back. "Your train is straight ahead and open to board whenever you're ready,"

"Thank you," Stella replied, snatching the papers before he could change his mind. She led Inge toward the train, placing a hand over her daughter's eyes when two officers roughly stomped by, gripping a young man between them.

"What was that for?" asked Inge, removing her mother's warm hand.

"I was just playing peek-a-boo with you," Stella said, laughing nervously.

"This is the last call for the train to Lausanne, Switzerland!" called the conductor, an impatient expression on his wrinkled face.

"Let's go, Inge, our adventure awaits!"

As they joined the line to board the train, a smile began to pull at the corners of Inge's lips, and before she could help herself, she started to giggle. *Why are we going to see Lausanne?* she thought. *It's Anne with lice! How strange!* Her laughter became uncontrollable, and Stella turned back to glare at her. Inge distracted herself by peering into the train windows, noticing that every passenger seat had a window. *Maybe this would be a great adventure.* She did her best daydreaming while looking out a window.

Once on the train, Stella led her past bustling compartments that were filled with large families and crying babies. The seats in this section were made of cold metal and allowed for very little leg room. There were five people per row, seated closely together, like sardines in a tin. Inge felt queasy as the scents of mold and sweat drifted through the congested rows of the coach section. She wished her mother would move more quickly.

When they arrived in the half empty dining room car, Inge could breathe again. The floors were squeaky-clean, not a crumb in sight, and the aisles were wide. Aromas of perfume and wine drifted through the air.

"Finally!" exclaimed Stella, taking a seat.

As Inge settled into her side of the table, she examined their fellow passengers, resting her gaze on a young woman across the aisle reading a novel. She noticed a white mink stole around the woman's neck and immediately heaved with disgust when she saw that the mink's head was still attached to the end. Inge scowled, but her view was suddenly blocked by an attendant in starched black and white.

"Good afternoon, little miss, Madame," the attendant said, bowing before the table. "We are offering a complimentary dinner for anyone with tickets for the sleeping compartments. May I get you something to eat or drink?"

"How wonderful!" said Stella. "We would love two *Tafelspitzs* and one glass of rosé."

"Superb choices! Your food will be ready shortly."

Inge curled her legs up onto her blue velvet seat and looked out the window. The train signaled its departure, and the sights of the platform were replaced by those of the city. Inge became mesmerized by the bright rays of sun streaming through the gaps between the buildings of Vienna. As Upper Belvedere Palace shaded the train, Inge marveled at how small the palace's visitors looked at this speed. It was difficult to distinguish between the living people and the statues of saints who protected the palace from their sites on the small limestone terrace.

As the train sped north through the city, Inge waited to catch a glimpse of her apartment building. She tried to ignore the fear that this might be her last look at her home. And then, there it was, eclipsed by St. Stephen's. *What is Omi doing? Is she already missing her family?* Inge was already missing her Omi. She gently passed her hand against the window as the cathedral came fully into view, as if trying to hold on to her past—even for one final moment.

The cathedral had watched her draw a heart for the stork each day; had heard her peals of laughter each time she chased Clara around the house; had chased away her boredom when Stella ran off to parties and dinners each evening. Inge knew that this final moment could be the last she would ever spend under its protection, and when the cathedral was no longer in sight, she grasped that she was leaving her past behind and rushing blindly into a new future.

In spite of her sorrow, a warmth had taken hold of Inge's insides, and she turned from the window to search for her mother's face. This was the longest time she had spent alone with her, and her heart felt full. Her mother was her idol, and when Inge looked into her beautiful brown eyes, she felt important. "How far away are we?"

Inge asked, pulling her napkin down onto her lap as she spied the waiter pushing a silver cart toward them.

"Not even remotely close. After we finish dinner, we will go back to our compartment to rest for the evening. Tomorrow, we have a long day ahead of us, so let's eat a plentiful meal and get a good night's sleep," directed Stella. "I do not know when we will get to eat again."

The only audible sound from the family's table was the clicking of their sharp utensils against the plates. Inge wondered where they would stay in Lausanne and thought about asking if it was their final destination, but she knew that her mother would never provide her with a clear answer. She finished her meal and turned her head back to the window. Emerald green hills had replaced the cityscape, and the vast, rolling fields soon pulled her to sleep.

6 NOVEMBER 28TH, 1938

LAUSANNE, SWITZERLAND

As Inge stepped off the train with her mother, the stark differences between this city and her native one struck her. In Vienna, people lined every corner of every street, yelling and rushing about, but in Lausanne, there was almost no one on the street. It was a wonder and a mystery to her.

After the lengthy train journey, all Inge wanted to do was find permanent shelter, but Stella grabbed her hand as they exited the platform and directed her to sit on a bench outside the station. Inge sat down and watched as pigeons flew down from the eaves and strutted toward them, looking for food. She was surprised when Stella crouched down before her, staring into her green, curious eyes.

Stella's model-like face was wet with tears, and passersby began to whisper and point. One elderly woman offered a handkerchief, which Stella used to cover her face in an attempt to mask her emotions from her daughter. Awkwardly, Inge patted the back of Stella's fur coat. This was the first time that her mother had displayed any sort of emotion in front of Inge, who didn't know how to respond.

Exhaling, Stella removed the handkerchief from her damp face. "I'm sorry, Inge," she said. "I had to spend all of our money on the train tickets and passports, so I can only afford to pay for our room. But don't worry, we will still eat a hot meal tonight."

Inge cocked her head in confusion. She had very little understanding of the concept of money and of the seriousness of the situation. However, one thing was clear: Stella did not want her to know what was wrong.

Stella stood up, brushing off her coat and collecting her leather suitcase in one hand and taking Inge's hand in the other. Together, they descended down the quiet streets of Lausanne.

They neared a limestone hotel, which commanded the attention of the street. Black woven metal balconies hung from the building's smooth, clean facade, and a statue of a pious saint stood above the grand arched entrance, protected on either side by two regal lions. Beneath them, the Swiss flag waved freely and proudly.

Pausing on the deep red carpet in front of the hotel's entrance, Inge clasped her hands together, flushed with excitement.

Stella shifted her gaze to the pavement when she saw Inge waiting to be led inside. She shook her head at her daughter, whose wide, toothy smile faded. This hotel would not be where they were staying for the night.

Turning off the main avenue, they reached their destination three blocks east. Deep cracks ran along each dull brick of the building's exterior, and its single wooden door was surrounded by cigarette butts, glass bottles, and debris. A disintegrated banner flapped lifelessly against the crumbling facade, which read *La Soupe Populaire*. With only the ability to read and speak German, the title of this building remained a mystery to Inge, who stared at a shoeless man lying on the dirty sidewalk in nothing more than a thin torn shirt and grimy pants. Inge trembled at the unfamiliar sight.

Once they stepped through the doors, the silent streets of Lausanne disappeared. Workers bellowed, children screeched, and the patrons inside the cupboard-sized restaurant yelled over one another.

Inge wrinkled up her nose to mask the foul smells of sweat and food drifting through the congested air. Hewing a pathway through the crowd, Stella found a place at the back of the long line that circled the walls. Stella was disgusted by the reality that she would have to feed her daughter in a soup kitchen, and her face turned red with shame as she watched her daughter's wide green eyes survey the room.

Inge searched the faces at the long table beside her. A ragged family huddled together at the end of the splintered wooden bench. The father's long, grizzled beard matched the frazzled hair sticking out from beneath the wife's headscarf. One of their children wore a shirt that extended beyond his knees while their other children's shirts clung tightly to their match-thin upper bodies. Inge wondered why they did not trade. Their sullen faces lit up when an older boy wearing a dirt-tracked top hat set food before them, and Inge realized how little food they had to share. She looked down and thought about her clean, well-manicured feet inside her freshly polished flats; turning her head, she looked at the teenage boy's torn, nearly sole-less shoes. Suddenly, her cheeks warmed with an overwhelming feeling of guilt.

"Next!" called the server behind the counter.

Stella pushed Inge toward a pile of metal trays that were streaked with mold and flecks of rotten food. Trying to ignore the unsanitary utensils, Inge trudged up to the food station. The kitchen was serving soupy mashed potatoes and burnt casserole; Inge felt queasy at the sight.

"I'll just have the potatoes, please. Thank you, ma'am," Inge called across the noisy butcher block, scrunching her nose as she stared at the food.

The volunteer rolled her eyes and slapped a large helping of pasty gray potatoes onto Inge's plate.

7 NOVEMBER 28TH, 1938

LAUSANNE, SWITZERLAND

After supper, Inge and Stella found a dingy hotel and approached the sleepy-looking woman sorting through a pile of skeleton keys at the front desk.

"Pardon me," said Stella, clearing her throat. "Is this Le Motel de Lausanne?"

"Yes, it is," replied the attendant in a bored voice.

"Very well. I was wondering if you have a spare single-bed room available for the night?"

"We only have singles," said the woman, picking up the first key in front of her. She eyed Stella's fur coat and expensive high heels. "Maybe you want the Hotel Royal Savoy Lausanne?"

"No, thank you. We would like a single room, please," replied Stella, her voice heavy with fatigue.

The woman handed Stella the rusty key. "All right then, third door down on your right," she said, chuckling. "The water closet is just beyond and watch out for rats in the hallway. I've already had a few complaints about them tonight."

Inge gasped and hoped the lady was joking. But as Stella unlocked the door to their room, a rodent ran past them, and Inge felt

it brush against her leg. The hairs on the back of her neck stood up, and she yelped, praying for her mother to hurry, hoping that they could close the door on all their problems. But Inge knew that was impossible as soon as she walked into the musty, damp hotel room, where the bedside table was stained, water dripped from the ceiling, and the sheets on the twin bed were blotchy with brownish, abstract shapes.

"It's been a long day, and we are exhausted," explained Stella, as if addressing her daughter's dread and doubt.

Inge nodded, too upset to say anything.

"I think we both could use some sleep," Stella continued, trying to sound optimistic. "We have another eventful day ahead of us." She wanted to make her daughter believe that she had a plan, that they would be safe, and that Inge could feel secure about their future. Yet, their life was changing right in front of their eyes, and there was nothing Stella could do about it.

As Inge lay in the bed beside her mother, she reflected on how different her life had been just the day before. Thinking about her apartment in Vienna brought tears to her eyes. She wondered if she would ever see Anna, Maria, or Marcel again. She had never been without them, so even in bed beside her mother, Inge felt alone. Her confusion and concerns about the future had not been quieted. *Where are we going? Who will help us?* No one had explained to her that the impending war would have such dire consequences.

Stella could feel her daughter's wakefulness, but she pretended to be asleep. She had kept so much hidden from Inge throughout her life for her own protection, and she would continue to keep her in a state of ignorance for as long as possible. There was no need to worry her about their uncertain future. Stella wanted Inge to believe that her mother had it all under control. She wanted her to believe that they were on a grand adventure, not fleeing for their lives.

And no matter the cost, Stella knew that she must shelter her from her true identity.

Inge could never know the truth of her Jewish heritage.

8 NOVEMBER 29TH, 1938

LAUSANNE, SWITZERLAND

The next morning, Stella and Inge left the hotel and slowly trudged along the cobblestone roads of Lausanne. The scenery shifted from quiet bakeries, clothing shops, and cafés to narrow, tightly packed apartments. The wails of hungry babies reached the streets, even through the small windows that were sealed from the brisk autumn air.

Stella stopped in front of a light green apartment building. Its bricks were worn and cracked. She wondered if the exterior had once been a deeper shade of emerald. Shaking her head at the distasteful building, Stella placed her suitcase on the ground and adjusted her coat.

Inge was staring hungrily ahead at a corner storefront, entranced by the delectable scents of cheese and meat, and she did not notice that her mother had stopped.

"Inge, come back!" yelled Stella, pulling her daughter out of her temporary hypnosis.

Inge turned and walked back. "Sorry, Mutti, I got distracted by the smell of real food," she said. "Like the food we used to eat," she added in a whisper.

Stella understood why Inge had been spellbound. Her cheeks flushed with shame, but she could not scold her daughter. They had not eaten since their dinner at the soup kitchen. Their stomachs ached, and their dull complexions were even more obvious in the daylight. Stella pursed her lips. She knew that if she waited much longer, the conversation she sought to have would not go well, so she kneeled in front of Inge. The cold ground pierced through her threadbare hosiery, and her hands began to twitch, a nervous habit of hers.

Noticing her mother's discomfort, Inge shifted her gaze back toward the delicatessen so as to not embarrass Stella. Their relationship had always been difficult. Inge desired to know everything while Stella was a private person who shut her daughter out, leaving her feeling unwanted and alone.

"Mutti, is everything all right?" she asked in a concerned tone.

Stella nodded and took a deep breath. "Inge," she began, "sometimes life doesn't always go as planned."

"I know, Mutti. Maria always said the same thing to me."

"Yes, but I need you to remember this during our conversation."

Inge's brows furrowed.

Contemplating how much to reveal, Stella bit her lip, sliding her white teeth along her red lips. She loathed demonstrating weakness, especially in front of her daughter, so she instinctively turned away, just as she had done throughout Inge's whole life. Stella stood and collected herself, releasing her daughter's hands. "Inge, I must leave for Paris tonight," she said cooly. "I have secured a position working as an opera singer's assistant, so I was able to get myself a visa."

Inge's heart rate quickened, and her rosy cheeks dimpled. She loved Paris almost as much as Vienna! The Eiffel Tower, exquisite food and restaurants, and lively energy of the French city reminded her of her home. She could already imagine living in a beautiful apartment overlooking Notre Dame Cathedral.

"Paris is wonderful!" Inge squealed, anticipating how their life would return to some sort of normalcy once they arrived. "That's not bad news at all, Mutti. I can't wait for our adventure to begin!"

"Inge, I think you misunderstood me," Stella said, blushing. "I couldn't get a visa for *you*."

Inge's excitement deflated, and her face fell. The words stung her like wasps. Living with Stella had already made Inge feel deeply lonely and misunderstood, so it was inevitable that her feelings would only grow without her.

Inge started to cry. "Please, please, Mutti, I will be extremely well-behaved!" she pleaded. "I must come with you, Mutti! Please! Please! You cannot leave me!"

"This isn't up for discussion," Stella replied. "Now stop making a scene."

Inge's palms began to sweat. Her mother had not explained anything about her future, and she had barely given her two days of her attention.

"But Mutti, where will I stay? And who will I stay with?" she asked, her voice cracking as she held back her tears.

Stella raised her arm and pointed to the entrance of a lime apartment building. "This is where you will live. A very nice Austrian family has offered to provide you with a room in their apartment for the next few weeks while I figure out how to get you to Paris. It was incredibly kind of them to open up their home to you, so please be appreciative and mind your manners."

Inge's face went blank. The aromas of meat and cheese faded, and the bicycles lining the cobblestones disappeared from her vision. All that mattered was her Mutti.

"But—" Inge started.

"Before you say anything," Stella interrupted and held up a finger. "I want you to know that I am doing this to protect you. Every place you go, every family you stay with, and every challenge you overcome while we are separated is to keep you safe. This is the only way. It is for the best."

Stella looked into her daughter's frightened green eyes, and for the first time in Inge's memory, her mother clutched her tightly in hopes of comforting her.

Inge trembled as she whispered in a small voice, "I wish you could stay. I'm scared. What am I going to do without you? I just want to be back home, not in a stranger's house in Switzerland."

Clearing her throat, Stella released her daughter. "Before I leave, I want to give you two things I brought from the apartment. First, some money—use this to buy food while you are staying here. And now for the real surprise: I brought you this because I want you to have a way to remember Vienna." She opened her purse wide. Inside lay a perfect china doll with a polished face, a white cotton dress, and black flats. She handed the doll to Inge, who immediately stroked its shiny red hair back from its face, just as she had when Stella first gifted it to her four years ago.

"Let this doll act as a reminder of your life in Vienna, and of your family," whispered Stella. "Hold on to it until we meet again. Goodbye, Inge. I'm going to miss you."

"Goodbye, Mutti. I'm going to miss you more," choked Inge as Stella backed away, turned and hurried down the sidewalk. Inge watched her until the brownish blur of her coat disappeared. Hesitantly, she opened the door to the apartment building, her precious china doll nestled under her arm.

9 DECEMBER 4TH, 1938

LAUSANNE, SWITZERLAND

Inge woke with knotted hair following a restless night's sleep, just as she had every other morning of her first week in Lausanne without her mother. She quickly dressed and left the apartment immediately after waking up to avoid disturbing the tenants. Walking the few blocks to a nearby bakery, she longingly eyed the trays of frosted and jellied pastries, knowing that she only had enough money for one plain croissant.

After breakfast, Inge embarked on her daily wanderings around the city, returning to the apartment only once the sun began to set. The family made it clear that she was an outsider, speaking in French in hushed tones when she was present and avoiding the front parlor where she slept on a dusty, sagging couch. Inge had never felt so alone. Even in Vienna, she'd had the staff to talk to.

One morning, just as the sun began to rise, a jarring honk startled Inge awake. Then, footsteps on the wooden stairs grew louder and louder until she heard a sharp knock on the apartment door.

The mother of the host family, who had yet to tell Inge her name, rushed into the front room and thrust the key into the lock. "Come in quickly," she said in broken German to the older man in a dirt-smeared shirt and black pants who stood outside. "No one can know you have been here."

The man entered. "I'm here to pick up an Inge Eisinger," he grumbled.

She nodded at Inge, whose heart started to pound viciously against her ribs at the sight of the man's thick black beard and ice cold blue eyes.

"Hurry up!" the man snapped with a menacing tone that jolted her from the couch. She frantically put on her coat, grabbed her small suitcase and beloved doll, and tripped to the door of the apartment.

"Thank you," she whispered to the woman, knowing that Maria would have been proud of her for remembering her manners.

On the road, the man prodded her into the back of an old car. The interior smelled like urine and eggs. Inge gagged, bit down on the collar of her coat, and closed her eyes, pressing her doll into her chest. She stroked her doll's hair, trying to distract herself with joyful memories of Vienna, Anna, and Stella.

They drove for hours through the rural countryside when the car suddenly pulled off into a wooded grove. Inge could barely make out the roofline of a small shack set back within the pine trees.

"Get out," grunted the driver.

Inge nodded her head, picked up her doll and suitcase, and stepped out into long, damp grass. It was not yet close to sunset, but the shadow of the woods cast the cottage into darkness. Inge's stomach felt sick as she closed the car door. It appeared that they were miles away from any other living people.

"Get inside," the man bellowed, kicking sticks and leaves aside to access the rotted front door.

Inge did not want to go inside. She did not want to be alone with this gruff stranger. A chill overtook her body, but she saw no other course of action and, steeling herself against the unknown, went inside.

"Sit," directed the man, pointing to a ragged chaise.

Inge positioned herself between two large tears in the cushions of the brown horsehair couch. She began to stroke her doll's hair again, singing softly to her, "O dear Augustin, Augustin, Augustin..." She could feel the man's stare as he leaned against a wooden table in the kitchen. He looked like a hungry lion waiting to pounce. Inge hugged her doll to her chest and began rocking back and forth.

A short time later, the man retired to the only other room in the house, and Inge weighed her options. Each hour with the stranger escalated her terror and feelings of dread, but she feared getting lost if she left the cabin. *Where will I go? What if there are wild animals in the woods?* Her worries paralyzed her, and her breath shortened into quick gasps. She closed her eyes, conjuring images of her mother into her consciousness.

The moist smell of chlorine infiltrates my flailing nostrils. I stare down at the shifting water and fight the urge to run away as fast as I can.

"Get in!" Mutti commands, wading into the shallow end.

The sea foam green of her swimsuit disappears beneath the water, and I reach for my swimming ring. As Mutti emerges, shaking the water from her curls, she wags her index finger at me.

"No Schwimmhilfe! *Get in the pool!" she orders.*

Huffing, I throw the ring onto the ground and stomp to the pool's sloped beach. Mutti doesn't love me, I think. She wants me to drown!

I tentatively enter the shallow end. The water chills my skin, even as I stand in the warm rays of the sun. Young children crowd the shallow water, and soon, my navy swimsuit is dark from the water being splashed upon it.

"Inge!"

There are so many people here today that I can barely make out Mutti's figure behind a group of boisterous, splashing boys, but she is there, waiting for me, her hands on her slender hips.

"Come, Inge," Mutti beckons. "I want you to swim to the end of the pool."

I shiver. I will surely drown, I think again, catching sight of my stricken expression in the clear blue water. Will Mutti be there to rescue me?

"Go on," she coaxes, coming toward me and laying a hand on my back.

Of course she will help me, I think, as relief washes the gooseflesh from my body, but just as I open my mouth to ask for her help, I feel a sharp pinch on my back.

"Swim or I will pinch you again."

I push forward, submerged to my chest, and begin paddling like I do with my ring on. But my body sinks lower, and I stand abruptly, wiping the water from my eyes. Mutti approaches and pinches again, this time on my right thigh.

"You must get your legs up," she directs, "and kick them vigorously."

"But Mutti —"

"Right now!" She points to the end of the pool, signaling that I must begin again.

Falling forward, my blue hands grope the water, and I lift my heavy legs. It is such a strain to get them moving against the water. I want to give up, but seeming to sense my reluctance to continue, Mutti pinches me on both feet at the same time.

My legs kick back against the pain, and I shoot forward in the water, finding myself in the deep end of the pool. Overcome by panic, my body goes rigid, and I start to sink. With my head under water, no one can hear my muffled screams. As water begins to choke me, I realize that I must save myself. I will drown if I do not start to swim. I open my eyes and see ringlets of red curls floating around my face. I am like a mermaid, I tell myself. I press my arms down hard against the water once, then twice. My head breaks the surface, and the rowdy sounds of the pool fill my ears. Breathing in, my chest burns, and I cough uncontrollably, but I keep kicking my legs and pressing my arms down hard. The edge of the pool is a couple of meters ahead, and I reach for it, kicking as hard as I can.

As my hands connect with the gritty concrete of the pool's edge, I realize that I am safe. I have saved myself. I start to cry, coughing and gulping air down into my lungs.

Mutti had taught me how to swim.

Inge opened her eyes as the man reemerged from the room beyond, this time reeking of wine.

"Get up, girl," he slurred. "It's time for you and I to get to know each other." Then, he was upon her. He ripped Inge's doll from her chest and grabbed both of her arms, lifting her off the couch and wrestling her into the bedroom.

Inge lay motionless in the back seat of the car, swallowing nausea down into the pit of her stomach as they sped through the darkness of the night. Her arms felt empty without the china doll, and she yearned for it. But after the man had torn the doll from Inge's arms, he'd forced her to leave it behind. Her heart ached to think of the gift from Stella, the beloved little doll with red hair that matched her own, abandoned on the floor of the filthy shack.

Eventually, the car left the even keel of the dirt road and stopped in a barren field. Sitting up tentatively, Inge peered into the black horizon, seeing nothing.

"This way," the driver mumbled as he pulled open the back door. "And don't make so much as a sound unless you want to be killed."

Inge shrank back. She wondered if she should try to run. Maybe he wouldn't find her in the darkness. But he grabbed her by the arm and pulled her out of the car, grunting, "Walk."

They tramped across the dark open field, pausing only when Inge asked to relieve herself. She was desperate to get away from her pursuer, but he suspected her ploy and pushed her shoulders.

About an hour later, she could make out faint lights ahead in the darkness. Walking closer toward them, she heard a whistle and realized that she was seeing the lights of a train station. Anticipation quickened her steps. Was it possible that she was truly getting away from this man?

Her body heaved in relief as they entered the station. Tired, worn-looking families huddled together around small suitcases. They wore utter despair on their faces, but Inge found comfort in their presence.

The driver suddenly grabbed her neck and steered her toward a platform, his rough hands stinging her cold skin. "This way!" he barked.

Following him to a train, he stopped and handed her two green sheets of paper. "Your papers."

"What are they for?"

"For the train. You are going to see your mother. That's what I was paid for."

Inge felt her lips pull into a cautious smile.

"This one's yours." The man pointed to the train and then turned back toward the entrance.

As he strolled out of the building, the faint smile left Inge's face and she curled her fists into two tight balls. How could Stella have left her with him? She would replay what he had done to her for the rest of her life, and she blamed her mother and herself. *Why didn't Stella find a way to take her along?* Inge fumed. *How could she have been so naive, thinking that strangers would protect her daughter just because she paid them?* She vowed that never again would she find herself at the mercy of a stranger.

"Miss, train tickets and identity papers," interrupted a man blocking the entrance to the train. Inge immediately recognized his gray-green uniform, and her heart beat faster—it was the same one that the men who had broken into her apartment and taken her father had worn.

"Miss, I need your train ticket and identity papers," repeated the guard.

Peeling her eyes away from the black cross embroidered onto his red armband, she handed him the papers with a shaky hand. He checked them over, and then stamped the pages.

"Where are you going, Mademoiselle Eisinger?" he asked.

"T-t-to see my mother," Inge stuttered.

He stared at her, and the vulnerability she had felt at the cottage returned. "All right, it looks like you are in the second to last row of coach."

"Thank you," she said. She wanted nothing more than to be safely ensconced inside the train.

10 DECEMBER 5TH, 1938
PIGALLE DISTRICT, PARIS, FRANCE

The train pulled up alongside Platform 9 of Gare de Lyon at 4 p.m. The chaos of the station pierced Inge's ears even before the door swung open. Stepping up onto her seat to see over the heads of her fellow travelers, she began a frantic search for Stella, but she could only make out strange faces beyond the train window. Once outside, Inge was trapped on the platform, which was flooded with travelers.

For an instant, she thought she recognized the pattern of her mother's favorite fur coat.

"Excuse me, excuse me," she said, pushing her way through the crowd, but the woman had disappeared. She stopped a conductor rushing by. "Pardon me, have you seen a woman named Stella with light brown hair and big brown eyes?"

The man shook his head.

Inge sighed. She reminded herself that Stella was always late, even to her own parties. But she always arrived eventually, breathless and beautiful. Inge stood fixed to the spot, willing her mother to appear.

"Inge? Inge Eisinger?"

She turned around sharply, whipping her red hair to the back, but she could not pair a face to the deep male voice calling to her.

"Inge! Inge! It really is you! Your Mutti sent me!" announced a tall thin man wearing a broad, welcoming smile and a frayed beige coat. Removing his beret respectfully, he revealed prickly bristles of light brown hair.

Inge shrank from this stranger—had her mother really sent another man for her? Panicked, she searched around her for an escape.

"It's okay, Inge. It's okay. There is no reason to be afraid of me. I'm Stella's—uh, your mother's—brother. I'm your uncle. She sent me here to collect you."

Inge instinctively looked up when she heard her mother's name.

"Wha- wha- what's your name?"

"My name is Emanuel Kupfer, but you can call me Uncle Manny if you like."

Anna had told her many stories about her son. He had left Vienna as a young man and traveled to Paris to work, then married and divorced a French woman. Inge noticed that he had the same creases on his forehead as her grandmother and the same deep-set eyes as Stella. She decided to trust him and cautiously took his outstretched hand. "It is nice to meet you, Uncle Manny."

"And you, Inge! I must say, you have grown so much since the last photograph your mother sent. I hardly recognize you."

"Will Mutti be meeting us soon?" she interjected.

His smile faded. Stopping in front of the exit, he crouched to look directly at her with worried eyes. "I'm so sorry, Inge, but your mother isn't able to see you right now. She has asked me to take care of you, though. I hope that's okay?"

Inge turned away as her lip began to quiver. "Of course it is okay," she said. "Mutti is busier than any other person I know, and I shouldn't be a bother to her right now."

"Don't you ever think that you are a bother to your mother. She loves you very much."

"It sure doesn't feel that way," Inge whispered.

"Let's go find our bus stop," he said, patting his niece on the shoulder.

Once they stepped off the bus, Emanuel placed his hat on his chest. "Welcome to Pigalle, my new home," he declared. "Make sure to plug your nose and stay close to me as we walk to the hotel. There are some dangerous people in this neighborhood."

Nodding, Inge stepped as close to her uncle as she comfortably could. They walked briskly down the debris-littered sidewalk, avoiding the women in brightly colored skirts and heavily rouged cheeks calling out to them in hushed tones.

As they turned a corner, the voices changed. More angry and impatient now, a group of distressed Parisians yelled at two criminals. Inge watched the melee in fascination; it was like a movie. She knew only how to say *hello* in French, but she could tell by the tones of the residents that the men were unwanted there. Manny grasped her elbow and led her across the street.

On the opposite sidewalk, the voices changed again, and the air was filled with unfamiliar Russian dialects. Inge noticed a large family huddling together on an apartment stoop, surrounded by bags and goods. Black scarves covered the hair of the women and girls. One, around Inge's age, wore nothing more than a thin brown dress in the chill December weather, tethered at the waist by a narrow rope. She spied a gold necklace with a small five-point star lying daintily on the girl's neck before their eyes met, and Inge looked away, embarrassed.

"Is that family homeless?" Inge asked her uncle, nodding backwards slightly.

"They are refugees from Eastern Europe, which means that they were not—uhm—accepted in their country, so they came here instead. Since they are starting a new life in a new country and cannot speak French, they must have encountered difficulty finding work, resulting in their unfortunate state."

Inge nodded, and Emanuel hustled her forward until they arrived in front of a rundown hotel. "I know it's not much," he said, "but it's affordable, and it's safe for people like us."

Inge forced a smile, pretending to understand. The peeling paint of the hotel's front reminded her of her first night in Lausanne with Stella, as did the putrid odor of mold in the lobby.

"Sorry for the smell," remarked Emanuel as they trudged up the stairs to his room.

Once they had arrived before a shabby door, Emanuel exclaimed "Welcome!" with forced jubilance and threw it open, revealing a small room with one single bed and one tiny window.

"But there is only one bed here," Inge blurted out before she could stop herself. "Where will I be sleeping?"

"I'm really sorry, Inge, but I can't afford anything more than this single room at the moment. I'm afraid this is the only bed, so we'll have to share it. Why don't you wash up a bit? Then we can turn in. You've had a long journey."

Inge set her suitcase down by the bed. After washing her face with cold water in the dingy basin, she climbed into the foul-smelling bed and positioned her body as close to the edge as she could. She tried to calm her discomfort with thoughts of home, but panic seized her when she remembered that she had known her uncle less than one day. She did not feel safe lying next to this stranger that her mother had sent for her. She did not feel protected. Inge barely slept a minute that entire night.

11 DECEMBER 22ND, 1938

PIGALLE DISTRICT, PARIS, FRANCE

Inge had been cohabitating with her uncle for three weeks, and in that time, she had somehow gotten used to the wretched sights of Pigalle. When she went outside, she steeled herself against the pleas from the gaunt, begging women and crying children. Refugees from German-occupied areas of Europe were fleeing to Paris by the thousands, and there was not enough food to go around. Inge could not understand the foreign languages, but she could recognize the hunger and desperation in their eyes.

Frequently, screams of terror would break through the night as guards from the French Republic pulled illegal Jewish immigrants out of their beds. There were two hotels in which immigrants hid, but they were only safe for as long as they could pay the police to turn a blind eye.

One morning, Inge was walking to the bakery when she was shoved off the sidewalk by a stern, menacing young officer.

"Can't you see we are working here?"

"S-s-sorry," she stuttered as she tilted her head up to meet his deep, fiery deep brown eyes. He held her back with a strong, stiff arm as a man with graying hair and disheveled clothes was pulled onto the street by two other policemen. "Somebody help me!" he pleaded, panting as he struggled to break free from the grip of the young officers.

"Shut up, you Jewish imbecile," growled one of them, flinging the man to the curb in front of Inge. She watched his eyes grow frantic before he plunged onto the hard concrete.

"Please, please! I will get the money!" he cried. "I will get a visa and become a citizen of France!"

A young woman burst from the door of the hotel. "*Vater, Vater!*" she whimpered when she saw the older man lying face down on the road. She ran to his side.

"No, Emilia, no!" he moaned. "Go back inside!"

One of the officers grinned as he pushed the young woman onto the ground beside her panting father. "Look at that, boys. Two for the price of one!"

"You little *juif* liars deserve nothing," snarled an older officer. "We have a spot for vermin like you at Rivesaltes." Nodding, he signaled for his compatriot to place the two under arrest, leading them to the back of a nearby police vehicle.

Inge watched the scene in horror. She could read the panic and anguish on the faces of these despairing refugees and wondered what crime they were accused of committing. They both looked so innocent. Why were these men arresting *these* refugees? The streets of Pigalle were full of homeless vagrants.

The menacing voices of the officers reminded her of the men who dragged her father out of their apartment in Vienna. *Had they committed the same crime? Is that why her father was arrested?*

Inge wanted more than anything to leave the police-infested streets of Pigalle, which haunted her with the ghosts of her past.

Back in the hotel room, Inge found Emanuel holding a crisp white envelope. He was startled to see her return so quickly, and he dropped it hastily into his shirt pocket. "Inge, was the bakery closed?"

"I thought we would go to breakfast together at the Russian restaurant," she answered, telling herself that the half-truth was okay because it involved spending time with him.

Emanuel's eyes dropped to the floor and his stomach rumbled. He had not eaten since lunch yesterday. "*You* may go down to breakfast if you wish," he replied, his gaze still fixed on the brown rug.

Inge frowned. She wondered why he emphasized that only *she* was going to breakfast. She decided that he must be joking. "Well," she chuckled, "When are *you* going to breakfast?"

As a hardworking man, Emanuel had the most pride of all the residents of Pigalle. He had tried to shelter Inge from their poverty by hiding his struggle to feed them both, but he did not want her to feel deceived, like she did with her mother. Anxiously scratching the side of his neck, he whispered, "Inge, I can't afford to pay for my breakfast anymore, and as a growing girl, it is much more important for you to eat than for me. So please go without me."

Looking at her uncle's worn, thin face, she was overwhelmed with guilt. Emanuel had already done so much for her. He should not have to sacrifice his well-earned meal—and before a grueling day of work as well. Inge hadn't known how dire his struggles with money really were.

"Uncle Manny, I can't take food away from you. It's your money—*you* should go down to eat."

Emanuel's face turned red, but with anger or embarrassment, Inge was not sure.

"Inge, I believe I made myself clear: I want *you* to go. Now please, go down before they stop serving." His tone communicated that the conversation was over.

Before exiting the small room, Inge turned back to her uncle and whispered, "Thank you."

Nodding, Emanuel pulled the envelope out of his pocket and waited for her to close the door.

Downstairs, Inge's food had just arrived when her uncle tore into the restaurant. "I have news," he said, waving the letter. "We are going to see your mother!"

Inge jumped up, knocking over the chair and ignoring the chastisements from the waitress. *Could it be? Would she finally see her mother?* "Are you sure?" she asked.

Emanuel nodded, and she hugged him fiercely, crying and thanking him repeatedly. Every day she had been with him in Paris, he had promised that they would see Stella soon, but they had not visited her once.

Inge could not contain her excitement. The moment she had dreamed about since Lausanne was finally here.

The lobby of the station at Pigalle was crowded with workmen in grease-stained clothing, and impassive policemen holding fierce German shepherds on leather leashes. Inge skirted the vicious dogs as she pushed toward the ticket booth.

The clerk scoffed at Emanuel in his threadbare overcoat and Inge in her frayed shirt, then nodded toward the policemen. The workers here turned a blind eye to the illegal immigrants of Pigalle, but only if they were paid extra not to alert the police. Their pockets might have been lined with the last remaining francs of the refugees, but they still acted as if the immigrants were less than human.

Inge frowned. Just one short month ago, she had been dressed in the same starched clothing as the clerk, but now people like him were repulsed by her. She wondered if she had ever looked at underprivileged people in Vienna this way. She hoped not.

"We would like to purchase two tickets to Champs-Élysée," Emanuel firmly said, ignoring the clerk's nod and flashing the stained, dirt-caked francs that he had pulled from his pocket. The clerk quickly handed the tickets to Emanuel as if afraid of catching an infectious disease.

Inge and her uncle walked briskly through the station, where rats scurried along the walkway and into hidden corners. Inge pinched her nose to mask the reek of urine and garbage. As they neared the train tracks, a small girl, no older than six-years-old, looked into Inge's eyes. Matted black hair covered her forehead, and bruises marked her stick-like arms. "Please, miss, do you have any food?" she pleaded, her chapped, cracked lower lip trembling.

Inge inhaled sharply. Her heart sank for the little girl, forced to live on the streets by herself. It brought her own situation into perspective. Even though Inge was hungry, she was not starving, and she was not alone. If she had food with her, she would have given it to the girl. Instead, Inge lowered her eyes and shook her head.

The small child forced a weak smile. "I understand, thank you." Then she turned her weary face to another stranger, burying her agony and hunger deeper inside of herself.

As the train rose from below into the 8th Arrondissement, Inge could make out the very top of the great arcades of the Arc de Triomphe.

"We have arrived in Champs-Élysée," announced the conductor.

"This is our stop," said Emanuel, beckoning for his niece to follow him out.

Stepping onto the platform, Inge's lips parted. She felt transported back to Vienna. The peaceful station was illuminated by bright lights, revealing wood-carved benches and jet-black ticket booths. One woman by the platform wore a beautiful green crepe dress with a pleated skirt that reminded Inge of a Japanese fan that her grandmother had bought her on a trip to Venice. Other women in pearls and emeralds flooded the platform, clutching elegant purses. Beside them stood men dressed in dark suits, with bright ties beneath their collars.

Once on the street, Inge took a deep breath, smelling flowers and hints of mint in the fresh air. She and Emanuel walked giddily along the prestigious Champs-Élysée, lined by cafés and shops hosting affluent families. Perfumed aromas wafted through the air. This square looked nothing like Pigalle.

"L'Hôtel California," announced Emanuel. "This is your mother's hotel."

Inge stood flabbergasted as she peered into a lavish courtyard decorated with pine garland and poinsettias. Smartly uniformed attendants opened and closed large doors while a glossy black car pulled up to the entrance, shining in the sun. A small fountain in the middle of the circular drive catapulted water into the air. Then, as if walking out of a movie, Stella emerged from the front doors, trailed by two cocker spaniels.

"Mutti!" cried Inge, running toward her.

Clutching the thin white leashes in one hand, Stella loosely hugged her daughter with the other. Inge noticed immediately that her mother's face had become thin and her mink coat had shed, but she still looked like a movie star.

"Hello, Inge. Now tell me, have you been well-behaved for your Uncle Emanuel since I last saw you? I do not want to hear that you have been acting up!"

"Yes, I have been on my best behavior. Oh, Mutti, I missed you so very much." Inge's eyes filled with tears as she grasped her mother's waist in another desperate hug.

"I missed you too, Inge," Stella replied, but she was already disentangling herself from Inge's grasp as the dogs tugged her toward a corner of the courtyard that they had been using as a bathroom.

"We have so much to catch up on!" Inge exclaimed, trailing behind her mother and the dogs.

"Yes, yes, I know," Stella said, "but I am afraid we cannot chat for long."

Inge stopped short. She wanted to let the dogs loose so that she could have her mother's attention for one minute; Stella appeared to care more about the dogs than her own daughter. "What do you mean?"

"It's my job as the opera singer's assistant. I must get back. Lucienne, my boss, thinks it is best if I terminate all relationships before next week, so I have to see you in secret—walking the dogs is my cover."

"What do you mean? What's happening next week?"

"That is actually what I wanted to talk to you about, Inge," called Stella over her shoulder. "The opera singer wants to escape the war, so she is moving to America, and she was able to get me a visa as well. However, family members cannot move without a visa. Next week I begin my life in America, but I'm afraid you must stay here. I'm terribly sorry."

Inge's face fell. Her mother did not appear to be terribly sorry at all.

12 DECEMBER 24TH, 1938

PIGALLE DISTRICT, PARIS, FRANCE

The bells of Sacré-Cœur rang high and clear outside the small window of the hotel room as crystal snowflakes drifted gracefully down. Inge could hear carolers' joyous songs renewing the streets of Pigalle. Yet for her, each song carried painful memories of Stella drinking wassail punch on the sofa, listening to carols on the gramophone, and watching Inge unwrap gifts. It was the one time of the year when Inge had her mother's full attention. Anna always hugged her fiercely as she tucked her into bed on Christmas night, whispering, "*Frohe Weihnachten!*"

Inge's eyes welled with tears, but she smiled in spite of her sadness as she watched a family dancing and singing on the street below. The young girl squealed with delight as her father spun her in the powdery snow. Placing a hand on the window, Inge made a wish that next Christmas would bring her family back to her.

She pushed her fists into her eyes to stop the tears and glanced around the empty hotel room. No evergreen tree dressed in candles and handcrafted ornaments; no silver garland strung over every threshold; no cheese plates, *Apfelstrudel, Palatschinken,* or cider. Ever since she had first stepped into the host family's apartment in

Lausanne, she had convinced herself that life would soon return to normal. Yet months later, she was living a lifestyle the farthest from normalcy she had ever been.

"I'm back," called Emanuel, brushing off his overcoat and removing his worn leather boots.

"Merry Christmas," Inge muttered in a very unmerry tone.

"It is indeed," said Emanuel with a smile.

Inge knew better than to expect Christmas presents from her uncle. He had skipped breakfast again that morning, and she knew that all of his money was being used to house and feed her.

"If you don't have work for the rest of the day," she asked hopefully, "could we go out into the snow? It reminds me of home."

"I'm afraid I have an obligation elsewhere."

"Oh, I-I understand, Uncle Manny," Inge murmured, casting her eyes back toward the window. She could still see her uncle's reflection in the glass; he was reaching into the pocket of his battered coat and pulling something out. He came up behind her, tapping her on the shoulder with one hand and carrying a surprise behind his back in the other.

"I know how hard it must be to be away from Mutti and Omi today."

Inge nodded and turned to face him.

"Well, I have an idea to cheer you up! Let's imagine we are inside our favorite movie. Mine is *Gently My Songs Entreat*, a film about a composer named Franz Schubert, so I will imagine that I am composing music as powerful as the songs in his collection *Schwanengesang*. Your turn!"

"You have probably never heard of it," said Inge tentatively. "And I've never seen it. But before we left Austria, my governess was going to take me to a Disney movie about a beautiful princess whose stepmother was a wicked queen."

"Oh, Inge, you underestimate me! The Disney picture in question is called *Snow White*!" he exclaimed, pulling out two cinema tickets from behind his back, revealing his "obligation."

Inge squealed with delight and grabbed the two tickets from his hand, reading the printed words in disbelief: Disney Presents Snow White. To her, the two pieces of paper may as well have been encased in gold, and she hugged them fiercely to her chest. Then, suddenly realizing the sacrifice that her uncle had made to purchase them, she responded regretfully, "But–but Uncle Manny, you shouldn't have. Th-this present is the most thoughtful and best Christmas present I have ever received, thank you, but..."

Inge meekly handed the tickets back to him, refusing to accept such a generous gift, but she felt his warm hands gently pushing back on her hands, and her eyes welled for the second time that morning, only for a much different reason. She was so touched by his love for her. In a short time, she had felt much more generosity and kindness from him than her own mother ever had. Emanuel had sacrificed his privacy and his meals. Now he had given her the best Christmas she could ask for. At that moment, she knew exactly where she was supposed to be.

"You deserve to be happy, Inge," her uncle said.

So do you, Inge thought. "You have done more for me than I can ever repay you for," she said sincerely, as her body filled with warmth, flushing out the dread for the first time in months. "You truly are the best uncle in the world. Thank you for everything. You deserve a lifetime of blessings, Uncle Manny."

13 JANUARY 28TH, 1939

PIGALLE DISTRICT, PARIS, FRANCE

Inge had been living with her uncle for a couple of months, and they had fallen into their own daily routine. Sometimes Emanuel picked up a short-term job, but more often than not, they spent their days walking throughout the district, Emanuel sharing childhood stories about Stella and Inge babbling about her unruly red hair, her bedroom window in Vienna, and pork fat. They occasionally played a game where they guessed how long it would take for Emanuel to find his next job, and whoever won chose their next outing in the district. When Inge won, she always led her uncle to the small park a kilometer outside of Pigalle that reminded her of the one Maria took her to nearly every day when she was young. To celebrate Emanuel's victories, he insisted that they continue to wander Pigalle in search of more jobs.

One evening, as they sat down to eat supper at the inexpensive Russian restaurant that they went to for every meal, Emanuel's face became grave. Setting down his utensils, he uttered, "Inge, I have big news to share with you." He could see anxiety in her green eyes, but he continued. "I have decided to join the Foreign Legion to fight against the Germans. At the end of the week, I will join a troop to help protect our country from the despicable Germans."

Years earlier, Emanuel's wife had joined the *Parti populaire français* and quickly became indoctrinated by their fascist and antisemitic beliefs, leading to the divorce from Emanuel. Although Emanuel was Austrian by birth, he felt passionate about fighting for France. It pained him to have Inge displaced yet again, and he worried that his niece would resent him for leaving her, but he knew in his greater being that it was his duty to join the Foreign Legion and help the cause.

Inge was shocked. She had no idea that her uncle had been harboring such a deep desire to protect his new country, nor had she known the depths of his bravery.

"A soldier," she exclaimed. "You are so brave, Uncle Manny! But... where will I stay while you're gone? I don't think that I should come with you. I would like to, but I think that it would be a little too frightening."

"Don't worry," he laughed. "You aren't coming with me, and you are much too young to join the Foreign Legion. Instead, I have arranged for you to stay with a kind host family here in Paris. They live in a big house in a beautiful neighborhood, and they even have a child around your age." Clutching his niece's hands across the table, he continued. "Please believe me when I say that I am certain they will take good care of you and treat you as if you are a part of their family."

Inge felt wretched. *This is even worse than becoming a soldier with Uncle Manny,* she thought. *Who are these strangers? What if they treat me like an outsider, like the family in Lausanne?*

She had just adapted to her life here with her uncle, and now it was about to change again. Wanting nothing less than to live with a new family, fear and anger and sadness began to overtake her.

"I will miss you," she whispered to Manny, and ran from the table, sobbing.

14 JANUARY 31ST, 1939

PARIS, FRANCE

Inge's host family lived in one of the most prominent areas of Paris, where it had become fashionable for the wealthy to host European children seeking refuge through the *Kindertransport.* After saying a tearful goodbye to her uncle, Inge hesitantly approached the beautiful brick townhouse, not knowing what kind of people she would find inside.

A maid in a crisp black-and-white uniform ushered her inside with a pleasant smile. The entranceway boasted elegant wallpaper, and a plush Oriental rug adorned the oak floor. Inge immediately removed her shoes, seeking to make a good first impression. She glanced to the left of the entry into a sparkling dining room, centered by a large marble-topped table surrounded by white, gold-trimmed chairs. In the parlor beyond, a glass chandelier with cut crystal that shone like diamonds hung above beautifully embellished floral sofas.

Following the maid through one opulent room after another, Inge felt increasingly out of place—and even more so when she was introduced to the dapper, polished Barclay family. She wore the same ragged cotton dress she had received for her eighth birthday and the coat that she had worn every day since she left Austria, though she now had to squeeze her arms into it. Although her shabbiness embarrassed her, the family seemed to ignore her appearance and graciously welcomed her.

"Inge, we are just so happy to have you with us!" gushed Mrs. Barclay, calming Inge's nerves. Her uncle had told her that the Barclays were a Jewish family from England, but she had not really understood what that meant and he had not known any more about them. Now, she saw that Mrs. Barclay's style resembled her mother's; she wore chic kitten heels, a bronze silk dress with puffed sleeves, and a string of creamy white pearls around her neck. This told Inge that the family lived as comfortably as she had in the past.

Extending a smooth, elegant hand, Mrs. Barclay continued, "I am Eleanor Barclay, and this is my son Michel. You will meet my husband at dinner. But you must be absolutely famished after your journey. Michel, darling, why don't you bring Inge to the kitchen for a snack before dinner?"

Inge followed her host brother down a set of spiraling stairs to the kitchen, staring at the back of his perfectly pressed waistcoat and coiffed brown hair. Her hand automatically moved to the skirt of her wrinkled dress, yanking at it in an attempt to smooth it out. She stopped abruptly at the bottom of the stairs as the boisterous scene from the kitchen overwhelmed her senses. Several white-clad cooks were finishing dinner preparations: one of them slowly removed a lobster from a paper bag and dipped it into a large pot; another tossed a fresh green salad with tomatoes and pearl onions. The yelling of instructions, clamoring of pots, and sizzling of boiling water flooded Inge's ears. She could only stare, dumbfounded, at the incredible spread.

Michel grabbed a baguette from a countertop and ripped off a piece, offering it to Inge as he eyed her with curiosity. He was an only child and tended toward shyness, so he was excited to have a new playmate living in his own house. Ever since he had learned weeks earlier that his family would host a displaced child, he had been fantasizing about building forts from bedclothes and sneaking late-night sweets from the kitchen.

Inge gobbled down the warm crusty bread. In Pigalle, she could only fantasize about eating like she had in Vienna. Now, the recognizable scents of fine cuisine overwhelmed her, restoring familiar feelings of content, comfort, and safety. As maids began to cart food trays up to the dining room, Inge instinctively followed, allowing herself to sink into the plush seat cushions that awaited her.

Introducing Inge as she sat down, Mrs. Barclay flashed her husband a dazzling smile and reminded him what an extraordinary gift they had been given. Mr. Barclay nodded silently in agreement.

Michel sat across from Inge, engaging her in polite conversation. Just as his parents had instructed him to do, his comments at the dinner table addressed the books he had read and the paintings he had seen, which told Inge that he was well-educated, maybe a bit boring. But as he spoke about these topics, his blue eyes widened with excitement and his enthusiasm made Inge smile, reminding her of her younger self. Because she only understood a few words of French, the family used hand motions and spoke in short, slow phrases as they dined, attempting to include her in the conversation.

The patriarch of the small family sat to Inge's right. Perched at the head of the grand table with his hands in his lap and his circular glasses balanced on his nose, Mr. Barclay represented a stoic philosopher, quiet and reserved. He rarely spoke at dinner, only adding to the conversation occasionally in a clipped accent. His stern eyes and serious demeanor made Inge fear that he might not want her there, so she looked into her plate when he spoke, eating voraciously to avoid responding to his comments. Although she had always been taught by her governess to act like a lady at the table, today she could control neither her appetite nor her nerves.

15 FEBRUARY 3RD, 1939

PARIS, FRANCE

"Are you ready?" Mrs. Barclay called up the stairs as she gathered the children's coats and shoes.

Inge reluctantly followed Michel toward the entryway. Today, she would begin schooling in Paris, which she was not looking forward to. Her French comprehension had increased, but she could neither write nor read the language, so she was to be placed in a remedial class. She lagged behind as the family climbed into a smooth black car.

Arriving at the large cobblestone school building, Mrs. Barclay led the children to a small classroom where five small square tables sat beside a blackboard. Inge gasped when she saw that the room was filled with colorful letters and picture books, realizing that the children in this classroom could not yet read. It was then that she noticed a large blue sign hanging above the door: *Bienvenue à la Maternelle!*

Inge's mouth dropped open, and she turned to Mrs. Barclay in alarm. "But Mrs. Barclay, I graduated from kindergarten in Vienna four years ago!"

Mrs. Barclay shrugged her shoulders and hugged Inge goodbye.

"I am so proud of you, Inge!" she whispered. "Now be a good girl and enjoy your first day of school."

Inge was left flabbergasted as Mrs. Barclay kissed Michel goodbye and trotted out of the classroom.

"Good morning, class!" announced a young teacher, entering with a big smile and a loose braid. "Let's begin today by sharing our name and our favorite color! I will go first: my name is Mademoiselle Sauveterre, and my favorite color is yellow. Now, our new student will take her turn."

Inge begrudgingly offered her name and favorite color, *violette*, then sat down, staring over the top of each of the other five-year-olds' heads.

Mademoiselle Sauveterre wrote three columns of words on the blackboard. "Today we will focus on learning to read and write the words found in our classroom: *le crayon*." She pointed to the word on the blackboard then to her pencil. "Repeat after me, class," she instructed.

"*Le crayon*," the little voices repeated in unison.

Inge cringed. She had never been so embarrassed.

After closing the morning's lessons with a picture book about a mischievous cat, Mademoiselle Sauveterre asked the children to take out their lunches. Just as Inge opened the brown bag that Mrs. Barclay had packed for her, a boy with dirty blond hair pointed at her and yelled, "*Grandmère*!" Before long, everyone except for Michel was laughing and repeating "*Grandmère*! *Grandmère*!" Even Mademoiselle Sauveterre could not hide her smirk. Inge miserably ran into the bathroom, where she remained for the rest of lunch.

16 OCTOBER 6TH, 1940

PARIS, FRANCE

Life with the Barclays became almost normal for Inge, and Michel became one of her closest friends. The family treated her like a daughter, and she quickly moved up to the fifth grade, her learning of the language fueled by the shame of her disastrous first day.

But the war finally reached Paris. The bombings began as if out of nowhere in June, and they grew louder and longer by the day. Any sensible person would realize that Paris was quickly becoming an unsafe environment for children.

Evacuations to the basement had become routine. The first siren sounded, and the housekeeper rushed the children down the dark steps; once the second siren sounded, an agitated Mr. and Mrs. Barclay would join them, sometimes carrying snacks and wine. In the chill of the damp cellar, the children would giggle at the fog of their breath and pretend to be dragons. Eventually, Mrs. Barclay would bundle them up with blankets, and Inge and Michel would curl up into small balls and fall asleep on the concrete floor. In the beginning, the family was able to exit and eat a late supper, but recently, they had been forced to sleep down below, listening to the sound of the air raid sirens deep into the night.

Early one morning, following a particularly late night spent in the shelter of the cellar, Mrs. Barclay called for the children.

"Inge, Michel, please come meet us in the kitchen," she said.

Inge crawled out from the entryway closet—her favorite spot for the games hide-and-seek she played with the maid and Michel—and joined the Barclays in the kitchen.

Trudging down the spiral staircase with her host brother on her heels, an unsettling feeling rushed through Inge's body. Her pessimistic side, used to let-down, worried that the Barclays were going to ask her to leave. But a moment later, her optimistic side grew excited, because she wondered if Mr. and Mrs. Barclay had possibly bought presents for the children in an early celebration of Armistice Day. Inge hoped the latter was true.

Standing next to Michel and across from Mr. and Mrs. Barclay, who had no presents with them, the children shared a skeptical look.

"Inge," Mrs. Barclay began, reaching her hand out to her host daughter's arm, "you know we have come to think of you as our own child, and we want you to be given the same opportunities as Michel."

"Thank you," Inge replied obediently, but she was starting to worry that this was their way of sending her off to another host family.

"We have some news that pains me to share with you both." Mrs. Barclay covered her face with a handkerchief, attempting to mask her red eyes.

"Take a deep breath and try again," consoled Mr. Barclay, patting his wife's hand.

Now the children shared worried glances.

Mrs. Barclay took a long, deep breath, closed her eyes, and continued, "We feel that the current bombings have made it too unsafe for you to stay in the city. There have been air raids almost every night, and I cannot bear the anxiety I feel that you won't survive the night, even in the bomb shelter. We do not want to keep you in this danger at such young ages, so we have made the decision for the two of you to reside at a British boarding school on the outskirts of Paris to keep you safe."

17 OCTOBER 20TH, 1940

MAISONS-LAFFITTE, FRANCE

Inge and Michel joined 300 other children at the British boarding school. Many were Parisians, from six years old to sixteen, escaping the restrictions to education under the Occupation, but others came from all over Europe.

The Barclay's driver dropped them at the school one frosty October morning, Inge and Michel huddled close together with their small suitcases as the student body amassed around them on the dewy green lawn. All they could see in front of them were the backs of the older students. The pair was electrified with nervous energy: Michel was excited to be away from home for the first time, and Inge, for her part, was eager to create real friendships with girls her own age—something she had never had in Vienna.

"Children! Please line up in front of the sign with your grade," commanded one of the teachers through a bullhorn. "We will begin announcements when everyone is in the right place. Hurry up!"

After hugging Michel tightly, Inge scurried over to the left side of the field where children her age gathered around a teacher holding a fifth-grade sign. She stood at the edge of the group, holding her suitcase behind her legs, trying not to look like a newcomer, and turned her attention to the podium. A formidable figure stood quietly waiting for the students to settle down.

The headmistress wore a dour black dress and a serious expression, her brown hair secured in a neat bun. "Good morning, children," she said. "I am Headmistress Brooks. It is my pleasure to welcome the new students who joined us this morning. Our school has long passed capacity, but we are honored to accept as many children as we can. The bombings and restrictions have decimated our city, so we welcome you with open arms!"

The faculty applauded, followed reluctantly by the other students.

"Because we now have so many newcomers, all students will be assigned a bedmate. If you are a new student, please report to your class teacher for your room assignment. Classes will be canceled for today as we welcome our new pupils. Now, be respectful and kind to one another!"

The students' applause resumed in earnest at this news, and they heartily cheered as Headmistress Brooks stepped off the podium. Inge followed her clambering classmates to the playground across the lawn and cautiously joined a group of fifth graders huddled in a circle beside the swing set.

"You will be a queen in our fighting game," instructed one of the boys to a girl with two pink bows on the bottom of her long blonde braids.

Inge examined the other girls who had also been appointed queen: each had shining blonde hair and bright blue eyes. The regular players were not as distinct as the queens; some had dirty blonde hair; others had brown or black. The torturers, the lowest-rung role in the game, almost universally had dark hair and dark eyes.

"Can I play, too?" asked Inge hopefully, making eye contact with the boy who looked like he was in charge.

The children turned to examine her, and it was clear that they struggled to categorize her bold red hair and bright green eyes. Huddling together in a closed circle, the boy conferred with the others. They hesitated to make her a queen, but where could they put her? The group decided that because of her wider figure and unusual characteristics, she somewhat fit the image of the grotesque torturer. She would have to start at the bottom and work her way up over time.

"Torturer it is!" exclaimed the boy, and burst out laughing. His friends joined in, cackling wickedly. Despite their teasing, Inge beamed. Just the act of being picked for something made her smile.

"I'm Roland, and I will tell you how to play the game," the leader coached. "There are two teams, and each team has a queen and a torturer. The queen rules the team while the torturer attacks and eliminates the people on the other team. The first to eliminate the opposing side's torturer and queen wins. We are on the left side of the playground, and the other is on the right. Do you understand?" Roland waited for Inge to nod, which she did readily, and then he scanned the crowd of players and pointed at two blonde girls.

The two queens screamed in unison: "Ready, set, go!"

Children scrambled to either side of the playground, and Inge rushed over to the other team's side. First, she went to a group of kids huddling beneath the slide. She did as she was told and scratched each child across their legs, pulled their hair, and escorted them out of the game—her duties as a torturer. Within a few minutes, she had become a master of her task, but she soon realized that the hardest part was avoiding the opposite team's torturer, who was the tallest and strongest girl in the game. Earlier, Inge had heard her yell her motto "No mercy!" while scanning the crowd with scrutinizing brown eyes and a malevolent sneer. Her bright laugh and playful braid might have deceived the other players—but not Inge.

It did not occur to the children, but the teachers who watched them play day in, day out noticed similarities between their students' game and the events unfolding in the world around them. It was clear that even if the children did not fully understand the events going on outside the walls of the school, they tried to make sense of the chaos of war through make-believe.

After a quick and bloody battle of that day's game, there were only four players left: the two queens and two torturers. The other torturer was huddling over her queen in an attempt to protect her, so she had her back turned to the field, which gave Inge an opportunity to eliminate her. As she snuck up, adrenaline rushed through her veins. Each step on the hard earth led her closer to victory and to proving herself worthy to her classmates. *This is my chance,* she thought.

Hands shaking, Inge grabbed the opposing torturer by her braid. The girl let out a piercing screech as she flailed her arms and kicked her legs, trying to escape Inge's grip. Inge led the girl onto the pavement of the playground to join the others who had been captured. As she released the girl's hair, a feeling of pride filled her. She had demonstrated that she was a worthy opponent.

"Good job, torturer! You just won us the game!" yelled Inge's team, rushing toward her from the field. A sea of sweaty pink-cheeked children engulfed Inge for a group hug, cheering as they embraced her. As the leader of the team, Roland rushed to join the celebration, but his shoelace had come untied, and he tripped in the mud, which only added to the messy, raucous moment of joy.

Inge's beaming smile was visible from across the field. She had not felt this proud since leaving Vienna.

18 OCTOBER 20TH, 1940
MAISONS-LAFFITTE, FRANCE

Inge was elated after her victory, basking in her celebrity status until bedtime when she retired to her room and found a small, timid girl standing there. She clutched a bag of belongings in one hand and twisted one of her pigtails with the other. The girl stood silently staring at Inge, who noticed that she was wearing a name tag with the name Lillian.

"Hi, I'm Inge, and I am new here too," she said, attempting to calm the young girl's fears. "What grade are you in?"

The young girl did not respond. She dropped her bag to the floor and climbed into bed fully clothed, turning toward the wall and curling up into a small ball. Inge shrugged and started getting ready for bed.

The next morning, Inge woke up shivering. *How had it gotten this cold overnight?* she thought. Rolling over, she realized that her nightgown was soaking wet. Shame washed over her before she remembered that she was sharing a bed with a very young girl.

Inge shook her bedmate's shoulder. "Good morning, Lillian, are you awake?" she cooed, trying to suppress her irritation. "There's no need to be embarrassed. We just need to get cleaned up."

"I can't help it. I'm only five years old," cried Lillian, covering her face with her hands, ashamed of what she had done.

"Please don't cry, Lillian. I know it's hard for you to be away from home. It's hard for me too!" Inge offered, patting her on the back. "Can you maybe wake me up if you have to use the bathroom and I will walk you there?"

"I-I can't control it, and I don't want to be attacked by the m-m-monsters outside," Lillian sputtered into her pillow with a muffled cry. "I wet the bed every night, even at ho-home," she stammered, looking up before breaking into heart-wrenching sobs. Inge stroked her head and tried to soothe her young friend, unsure of what to do.

The following night, and every night after that, Inge slept on the floor.

Indistinct hollering echoed off the pale walls of the dining hall as Inge entered for breakfast later that week. Rubbing her sleepy eyes, she located Michel sitting at the end of the second long wooden table.

"Gooooooooood morning," she yawned.

"Inge, you look terrible! Why are you so exhausted?"

Before she could answer, she felt a tug on one of her curls and whipped around to see Roland smirk at her before taking his reserved seat in the middle of the main table.

"He's such an *imbécile.* I hate him," whispered Michel.

"I hate him too," Lillian, who was sitting next to Michel, parroted in a quiet voice. She smiled shyly at her new friend.

"Everyone does," proclaimed 13-year-old Marguerite, rolling her eyes as Roland removed his cap and pushed a lock of shining blonde hair from his forehead.

"Correction," a queen from the torturer game added. "Everyone except Headmistress Brooks."

"Well, of course she doesn't hate him," retorted Louis as he scratched his nearly bald head. "He's her son!"

"It isn't fair," Inge huffed, turning to her dry rutabaga. "Roland should be treated just like the rest of us." She grabbed roughly at the newly short red curl he had touched, seething in her seat. Although she disliked her hair color, one aspect of her hair that she had enjoyed was its long length—but now it was cropped, thanks to a dictum from the headmistress to curb the spread of lice. Her shoulders and cheeks felt bare and exposed, and she burned with resentment. "We girls should not have to have shorter hair than he does," she continued bitterly. "Why should he be exempted from the rules?"

"The same reason why he is the only student who has his own bed: nepotism," said Marguerite, pulling at her own ear-length golden strands. "It isn't fair, and I think we should do something about it." Before the mandate, her hair had reached almost halfway down her torso, so she was just as incensed as Inge by the previous day's events. "For all we know, Roland could have started the outbreak of lice, which means that the required 'cleanliness' haircuts could have all been for nothing," Marguerite fumed.

Glaring at Roland, who sat with an innocent expression among the staff, the children shook their heads.

"Shush," Inge said and placed her index finger to her lips, lifting her chin toward the aisle as Headmistress Brooks approached their table. The students fell silent and bowed their heads down to their plates.

"Mr. Barclay, how many times must I remind you to hold the fork in the English way?" the headmistress spat, pursing her lips.

"Pardon me, Headmistress," said Michel.

Lillian grabbed his elbow under the table in fright.

"We must maintain our manners in the face of the monstrous Germans, children. If we allow them to take our dignity, we have lost this war."

"Yes, Headmistress," the children responded, and Michel made a show of turning his fork backwards to please her. They let out a collective sigh once she was out of sight.

"I almost—" Michel was interrupted by the sound of a blaring alarm, and the children began to rise and filter into the aisles.

"Follow the bomb protocols, children," shouted the headmistress. "Use your protocols from our drills!"

The teachers in the dining hall rushed to the back of the hall and threw open the wide double doors. Covering their ears, the students rushed toward them.

Running alongside Michel and Lillian, Inge instinctively grabbed their small hands and followed the crowd of clambering children. *Didn't the Barclays send us here so that we would be safe from the bombs?* she thought, her mind spinning. The adults yelling orders and the nervous voices of the children around her became blurred as she felt a small hand slip from her own. Turning abruptly, she saw that Lillian had stopped, frozen in place.

"What's wrong? We must go!" Inge yelled and was nearly knocked off her feet by the stream of children racing in the opposite direction. "Lillian!"

"Every student must have a gas mask! Quickly!" shouted a teacher from nearby.

Leaving Michel next to the teacher, Inge fought her way back to Lillian and picked her up, feeling a familiar wetness seep into her uniform skirt as she carried her young roommate back to Michel.

Inge instructed him to get three gas masks and reminded herself of her priorities: protect the little ones and survive. In order to do so, she needed to get them out of the building. Older, stronger students had already pushed their way outside. Still carrying Lillian, Inge grabbed Michel's hand once again and pulled him toward the exit.

"Follow the crowd to the main field," directed a teacher standing outside the doors.

Inge saw that the edge of the field farthest from the school was lined with students. Since the Germans targeted buildings, they needed to evacuate quickly and camouflage themselves against the dense forest bordering the school.

"Michel, put on your gas mask then run to the others," Inge commanded, struggling to pull on her own mask with one hand as Lillian clung to her and sobbed.

Every student in line looked identical in their black masks and short hair. The only difference was that some wore skirts, and some wore pants. Teachers zigzagged between the lines, checking that the attachment straps wrapped tightly around each child's head and did not impinge the exhalation valve. Hearing the whir of plane engines, Inge's breath quickened, but as she breathed in, the rubber of the mask suctioned onto her face, making it very difficult to get air. She began to feel light-headed as her vision darkened, and she wondered if she was having difficulty breathing or if the blitzkrieg had begun.

Lillian clutched her tighter and cried harder as the planes approached. Inge knew that she must calm her friend, and she focused her blurry vision. Stroking the young girl's cheek, Inge attempted to console her. "It will be alright. We are safe out here."

"Look, Lillian, I am a pig!"

The girls stared at Michel as he started snorting inside his mask.

"That's right, you are!" Inge giggled, her breathing slowing. "Look at your dirty snout!" She grabbed at the black exhalation valve on his mask, and Lillian started to laugh. A teacher lifted her from Inge's arms and carried her closer to the woods where the other kindergarten students huddled together.

Michel's smile faded, and his voice grew high and loud as the planes of the German Luftwaffe materialized overhead.

"I'm scared, Inge," he cried. "I don't want to die. What if they bomb us?"

She hugged him tightly. "They won't. I'm scared too, but I-I think we are safe here."

"What if we aren't?"

Grasping Michel's face in her hands, she looked into his eyes. "We survived the bombings in Paris by staying together and being brave, remember?"

Michel nodded.

"I know we will survive these bombings as well. We have to," she added.

19 MAY 17TH, 1941

MAISONS-LAFFITTE, FRANCE

It was a cloudy day in the outskirts of Paris, but Inge, Marguerite, and Michel decided to go out to the field anyway. As they stepped outside, the moist humidity instantly frizzed Inge's unruly hair.

Fog hung from the clouds, encircling the school and secluding the students from the outside world. Inge preferred to stay on the swings because running through the thick mist made her nervous, but the other fifth graders wanted to run through the fog instead of playing at the playground with the younger kids. So, Inge joined them; she did not want to diminish her high standing with her friends.

"On your marks, get set, go!" everyone yelled in sync.

Inge felt unbalanced as she ran, sliding across the wet grass in her ballet flats. Edging farther away from the playground, her surroundings became even less visible. She could hear the boisterous voices marking the finish line and sprinted toward them, but Inge slowed as a stooped figure appeared through the fog. She could make out the silhouette of an old woman, wearing a long dress and holding a bag by her side. The figure approached, taking one careful step at a time.

"Inge?" questioned the hunched form, her voice heightening as she enunciated the *e*.

The soothing, familiar lilt of her voice stopped Inge in place, and her kind features became clearer through the mist.

"Omi?" she asked.

Anna reached for her. Her short gray hair blended in with the fog, and Inge thought that she might actually be a ghost. She wore the same loving, softly wrinkled expression that Inge dreamt about each night, however, and she embraced her without hesitation.

As Anna held her tightly in her soft, delicate arms and stroked her head, Inge finally felt completely safe and protected. She was overwhelmed by how comforting it was to no longer be alone, to be with her family who would make everything okay—even if that person wasn't her mother. Standing there, secure in Anna's arms, Inge saw her in a new light. She had watched Anna struggle for independence her entire life under the control of men, and as she held her there and whispered how much she loved her, Inge realized that her grandmother was her hero.

Anna looked into her eyes. "I can't believe how much you have grown!" she said. "How are you, my love?"

"I've been all right, Omi, but I missed you so much. It's been difficult to adjust to living by myself."

"Oh, Inge, I am so sorry. I know how hard it must have been for you, but you are so brave. I missed you dearly. I want you to know that you will never have to worry about being alone again."

Inge barely dared to ask. "Am I going with you?"

"Yes, my dear, I didn't travel all this way just to lose you again! I came to get you so that we can continue this journey together."

"Oh, Omi, is it really true?"

Anna nodded and closed her eyes as if she was imagining their future together.

Inge felt so incredibly relieved that she lay her head heavily back down onto Anna's chest. Grateful tears spilled from her eyes as unkind images of Lausanne and Pigalle ran through her mind.

After many silent moments passed, heavy with emotion, Inge lifted her head and wiped her eyes. "What will we do on this journey? Where will we go?" Praying that she would say America, Inge envisioned her mother coming to them, joining in their embrace.

"I want to bring you with me to a tiny village with farmlands in Central France. It's called Buxières-les-Mines. We will leave as soon as possible. We are taking one of the last trains that will leave Paris for a while, so we must hurry."

Inge wanted to know all about Vienna and if Anna had heard from Stella, but her grandmother's face was solemn and worried, so she decided to return to her dormitory to collect her things right away and say goodbye to Michel, Lillian, and Marguerite.

Crossing the short distance through the front field and playground, Inge called goodbye to a group of children.

"Goodbye, Inge!" they responded, barely looking up from their games. They had grown used to their friends leaving.

"Have fun finding another torturer for your game!" Inge teased as she pushed open the grand wooden doors of the school for the last time.

20 MAY 17TH, 1941

PARIS TO BUXIÈRES-LES-MINES, FRANCE

The road to the train station was mostly empty, except for a few children playing outside their houses where their mothers were pinning laundry onto lines. Inge wondered how long the ladies would be able to keep their laundry clean before a bomb exploded.

"Inge," Anna interrupted, "have you heard from your mother?"

"No, not since before Uncle Manny left last year. Have you?"

"No, I am sorry to say that I have not. After you left, Vienna became increasingly unsafe. SS officers paraded through the streets, pulling unsuspecting citizens from their homes. August Wagner, our dear neighbor, was arrested by the Gestapo for his affiliation with the church, never to be seen again. Poor, poor Frau Wagner. You should have seen her sorrows, Inge. And it was probably someone in the building who reported him to the Nazis. It is a bad time for Austria. Many of our friends joined the party—such a disgrace! I no longer knew who to trust, so I left the apartment, and I have spent the past year trying to leave the country and get back to you. I have been on quite the adventure, my love."

"Omi, I had no idea!" Inge wrapped an arm around her grandmother's waist. "I'm sorry that I was not there with you."

"Oh, Inge, what kept me going was knowing that you and your mother had made it to France! I tried escaping Austria through Alsace Lorraine twice, but both times, the French troops sent me away for not having a visa."

Inge gasped. "How awful!" She knew those feelings of rejection and disappointment. The scene from L'Hôtel California replayed in her mind.

Noticing her granddaughter's downcast look, Anna decided to keep the rest of her ordeal private. "But why don't you tell me about your journey from Vienna?"

"No," said Inge forcefully. "I mean... you haven't finished your story yet, Omi. I want to hear the rest."

Anna glanced sideways at her granddaughter, recognizing that their journeys might have followed different paths but shared many of the same hardships.

"Well, I returned to Vienna to see about buying a visa. We could no longer go through the proper government channels. The Nazis control everything now." She shook her head. "Luckily, your mother had left a contact for such a thing, but I knew it would be costly. I sent a message as she had instructed, then I walked to the Rennbahnweg District the next night."

Inge stopped and stared at her grandmother. "Alone?"

Anna chuckled. "I dare not endanger anyone else!"

She paused, remembering her fear as she had turned into the cobble-stoned alleyway swathed in darkness. As uninviting as it had appeared, desperation had pushed her forward.

"I was meeting your mother's, ah, acquaintance, Dominik," continued Anna. "He had a visa for me, but he wanted to be paid."

Anna thrust out her left hand to Inge, who immediately noticed the absence.

"Your ring!" she cried. "Not Opa's ring!"

Nodding, Anna brought her naked hand to her mouth, stifling a sob. She had not intended to tell Inge of this heartache, but it was such a relief to share the burden with her. "Yes, I am sorry to say, I was forced to part with my wedding ring." She had worn the one-and-a-half-carat diamond every day for over 30 years, and she remembered how her hand was visibly shaking as she placed the ring into Dominik's hand. She had immediately had the urge to snatch it back from his grasp and run, but she knew that the visa would be her only route to escape.

"I'm so sorry, Omi," Inge repeated.

"I know, my darling." She cupped Inge's face in her hands. "But getting back to you was worth all of my jewelry, and I know Opa would have understood."

The two embraced, both acknowledging that the losses they had suffered were not as great as their love for each other. Now they had found that love again.

"Now we need to hurry, my darling. We cannot miss our train, or we will be sleeping in the station overnight. Let us go." Anna rubbed her granddaughter's arm, and they resumed their walk toward the city.

Gare du Nord station was nearly as deserted as the roads outside. The platforms for the southbound trains were empty. No one was traveling into Paris anymore.

"Last call for the noon train to Gare de Moulins Sur Allier!" yelled the conductor, peeking his head out the train window. Anna and Inge stepped into the overcrowded car together, clutching their bags and holding each other's hands. Inge squeezed Anna's hand extra tight.

The train slowed, signaling their arrival into their new town, and Inge sighed. She wondered how many more miles she would travel away from Vienna. She gathered her coat and suitcase, paused to make a wish that this new village would bring them peace, and followed Anna off the train.

Once her eyes adjusted to the bright sunlight, she could see only endless green fields, interrupted intermittently by a graying wooden barn. The lowing of cows replaced the honking of city cars, and her hopes of finding a life similar to her past were crushed once again.

Anna approached the clerk at the depot. "Two bus tickets to Buxières-les-Mines, please," she commanded, handing the bus driver four centimes. "Less than 100 people live in the village we are traveling to," she said once she had their tickets.

"How many live in Vienna?" Inge asked.

"Around 1,700,000 people lived in Vienna before the war," Anna replied. She turned abruptly toward the approaching bus so that Inge could not see the fear in her expression. Anna was afraid they might never return to their home.

As the creaky bus rushed into the countryside, leaving a dense wall of dust in their wake, Inge lay her head on the cool windowpane. The fields blurred together like an endless shaggy green carpet. Her eyelids softly shut, and her mind drifted back to her old school, wondering who had taken her place as torturer. Inge realized how much she already missed the friends she had made there, Michel and Lillian most of all.

About 30 minutes later, Inge woke up as the bus rolled to an abrupt stop. "This is it," announced Anna. "Welcome to Buxières-les-Mines, Inge!"

They stepped onto a dirt street in a provincial village. Two men peered out at them from a rundown mercantile shop, but besides their suspicious stares, there were no other signs of life. They passed a number of boarded-up shops—a dress-maker's, a bakery, and a café—and Inge wondered how they would eat without basic goods available. Eventually, they came to a café door flanked by two black umbrellas that stood like doormen signaling their welcome. Across the street, a wide green awning over a nightclub announced that it was also open. *Petit Casino* was written in red script above the entrance.

Nearing the edge of the one-kilometer-long village, there was one more shop. *Boucherie,* read a fading wooden sign outside the storefront. The bell on the door chimed, and a young girl around Inge's age exited the shop. She carried a small, wrapped parcel in her left hand and a bucket of water in her right as she turned toward the vast swath of farmland. *She must live out there,* Inge reasoned, *but where?* She could not even see a house among the rolling fields.

Anna woke her from her thoughts, dropping her suitcase in the dirt in front of a worn two-story building. "We're here!"

Inge stepped back to look at the house, and her heart began to swell. "Omi, this is an amazing house!" It was the biggest dwelling they had passed in the town so far, and it looked far more welcoming than her uncle's apartment building in Pigalle.

"Yes, it is a very pretty hotel," Anna corrected. "We were lucky to find an affordable room here."

Inge sighed, deflated. She had hoped that the entire building would be their new home.

They entered the hotel and Anna spoke to the hostess, who handed her a key and pointed to the right.

Resigned to yet another new dwelling, Inge followed Anna down a narrow hallway, running a hand along the cracked, cream-colored walls. Inside their room, a single bed was in the center of the miniature-sized room.

At least my new bedmate will not soil our sheets, Inge thought.

21 MAY 18TH, 1941

BUXIÈRES-LES-MINES, FRANCE

The next morning as Inge's eyelids fluttered open, Anna announced that she would begin instruction at the village school immediately. "I want you to start today so that you don't fall too far behind. Get dressed, and I will prepare your breakfast. Did you notice that the schoolhouse is right across the street?"

Inge nodded reluctantly. She did not want to leave her grandmother after having just found her again, but she knew better than to argue. Without enthusiasm, she dressed for school and ate some dry oatmeal.

Several other children around Inge's age pushed and jostled through the front entrance. Upon entering, she realized that the school was only one room. *But how could all of these children be in the same grade?* she wondered.

Inge greeted one of the young students sitting in the front of the room, who then pointed to a wobbly table in the back intended to seat eight small children yet overwhelmed by five large boys and six girls. The girls sat on a short bench on one side of the table while the boys piled haphazardly onto a bench on the other. They surrounded a small boy in the middle who rocked and fiddled with his shirt, unbuttoning and refastening his top button. His disheveled look made him stand out from the group, and when he felt Inge's eyes on him he nervously moved his hands from his shirt to his mouth, biting his fingernails while turning his gaze to the ground.

Inge sat down on the half-meter of empty bench extending from the end of the girls' side of the table.

"I'm Inge," she whispered to the girl sitting next to her. "I've just arrived. What's your name?"

"I'm Renée!" the girl exclaimed. She wore a jumper printed with small bouquets of irises, and Inge knew that Renée was someone she wanted to be friends with.

"My name is Jeannine," called another girl sitting at the table.

"And I'm Claude," stated the boy sitting across from Renée wearing stained trousers and muddy boots. Inge assumed that he had traveled in from one of the farms.

"I'm Thomas," whispered the nervous, dark-haired boy in the middle, who then returned to biting his nails.

"Wait, Inge sounds like *singe*!" yelled out a boy named Léon, grinning.

Inge's cheeks flushed red at the boy's comment about her name sounding like the French word for *monkey*. In German, the "I" in Inge was pronounced as an "I," but the French children pronounced the "I" as an "A," and Inge despised the way it sounded. She hoped no one else had heard him.

"Yeah, she even looks like a monkey," Léon continued. "Look at her red hair and freckles!"

A couple of the boys began scratching their bellies and screeching like monkeys, but a glare from a tall thin man who had just stormed inside the schoolroom brought a dark cloud, and the table fell silent.

"Good morning, everyone," said the teacher.

"Good morning, Monsieur Dubois," they responded, and rose. Inge followed. They placed their right hands over their chests and pledged allegiance to Marshal Pétain, the savior of France. Inge had only heard his name mentioned in snatches of adult conversation, so she was not sure if he could actually save them from the Germans, but she followed the lead of her peers regardless.

"We have a few announcements for today," muttered Monsieur Dubois after the pledge. "First, there is a new student joining us today—again." His irritation was clear, although he stopped short at rolling his eyes. "We therefore need a refresher on the policies for new students. Our school rules are simple. There is no speaking while school is in session unless you are instructed to speak. And our second and final rule is that you must stand up when speaking to me. Displaying a lack of respect to a teacher will result in punishment," he warned, pointing at the ruler on his desk. "School finishes when children reach the age of 14 and they receive their *Certificat d'Études Primaires*."

As he spoke, Inge prayed that she would not be there until she was 14. Even if they stayed in the village, she knew that she would have to find a job to help support Anna and herself. Although her grandmother's will and determination were strong, Inge had noticed that she now moved with a pronounced limp and needed a break after just a few minutes of walking.

"I need everyone to hand me their assignments that were completed overnight," the teacher continued, walking to the back of the room to begin collecting assignments. He carried his ruler with him, tapping it against his leg as a sign of intimidation. Inge disliked him immediately.

Monsieur Dubois reached the back table and counted the assignments he received. Pausing, he recounted. "Who did not complete the assignment?" he spat out.

Everyone looked at Inge, and her face turned a deep crimson.

"My apologies, Monsieur Dubois, it was me," Inge said. "I just moved here, and I was unaware that there was an assignment due." She quickly added, "I would be happy to make up for it, as well as any other work you believe would be suitable."

Monsieur Dubois *tut-tutted* and shook his head as he proceeded to the next table. Gulping, Inge committed herself to finding a way onto his good side.

That night, Anna watched Inge with concern as her granddaughter pursed her lips and stared out the window of their small room. Anna could only guess at what was worrying her: school, the war, her mother's whereabouts, or any of the incidents that occurred before Anna had found her at the boarding school. Her granddaughter had not mentioned anything about her journey, and Anna was very worried about what had happened along the way.

"Omi?"

"What is it, Inge?"

"I was just curious as to why you picked this village. I heard a classmate say that it is not even on the map!"

"I found it when I was staying at a rental room in Paris," explained Anna. "The couple I booked it with told me that they were from a small village in the middle of France. After talking to them, I thought it was our best option." Anna left out her real motivation: that the village was unoccupied and safe for them as Jews. She wanted to respect her daughter's wishes and shelter Inge from the truth about her identity for as long as possible.

"I'm going to get started on our dinner," said Anna, changing the subject as she meandered over to the window. She winced from the ache in her tired left hip. "But I have something to give you first."

Inge shifted her gaze. She did not want her grandmother to know that she was aware of her pain. Anna had always been so proud and vibrant, and Inge did not want her to feel diminished.

Anna put her warm hand on her granddaughter's shoulder and gently turned her back around. "I wrote to Mutti to tell her where we would be staying, and this was waiting for us when we arrived at the bus depot."

Inge's demeanor instantly lifted as she snatched the letter from

Anna's hands. She ripped open the letter and drank in her mother's words, reading and rereading. It was many minutes before she remembered her grandmother's presence.

"Oh, Omi, I'm sorry! It's just that it's been so long since I have heard from her. Here, you can read it too."

"You keep it for now, my love. I will read it after dinner." Anna patted her cheek.

Inge suddenly felt selfish for wanting to be reunited with her mother while Anna was sacrificing so much to take care of her, yet she could not help imagining the grand apartment her mother probably inhabited in America. Being reunited with Stella was her constant daydream. Inge craved a similar life to the one she had had in Vienna, even though this most recent move seemed to have made that impossible.

At the alcohol burner, Anna was pulling out two bags, one filled with beans and the other with a nearly invisible amount of salt. Mixing them together in a tin canister over the burner, she prepared their dinner. They could not afford to buy tasty ingredients like olive oil or pepper, nor did Anna have access to a proper stove, so she had to become creative. She mixed the food together with an old, rusted fork that the hotel had given her and used water as a substitute for oil. She then plated two small portions of beans and brought one over to her granddaughter with a weak smile.

"Thank you, Omi, it looks great!" fibbed Inge, investigating the plate. The boiled beans smelled of burnt firewood, so Inge did not want to eat them, but when she saw her Omi gobbling them down and looked into her big somber eyes, she knew she had to make the best of the situation.

As they dressed for bed later that evening, having just returned from the communal, outdoor bathroom Inge's thoughts wandered before returning to her life back in Vienna.

. . .

I-N-G-E, Inge, Innnnnnge. The way my name sounds does not settle well on my tongue. I try pronouncing it in different ways to make it sound like a normal eight-year-old girl's name, but it never sounds right. The other girls in my class have beautiful names like Elisabeth and Sophia. All my name does is make me stick out like an underdressed guest at one of my mother's dinner parties. Well, that, and my infuriating red hair and green eyes. I look different from all my friends with their classic blonde or brown hair, and it frustrates me. Mutti is the reason for my differences, but I suppose that's the thing with Mutti, she likes being unique.

I cover my ears with a plush white pillow as Mutti and her friends listen to a group of unbearably loud live musicians. When will their infernal ruckus finally be over? I've been trying to sleep for at least two hours. I have never met anyone else who listens to music at such an ear-splitting volume.

After enduring the same intolerable off-pitch voice for another 20 minutes, I decide that I have had enough. I put on my ballet shoes and tiptoe over to the dining room, praying that Mutti won't notice me on my way to the forbidden kitchen. I have been dreaming about pork fat on black bread with salt for the past two hours.

My journey across our hallway feels like miles; I move so slowly that my toes begin to ache, but I am determined to taste the delicacy I have been smelling all evening.

I arrive at the kitchen, my favorite room in our entire apartment, and cautiously enter. The walls are painted bright white and accented with small, colorful flowers. The room always smells of pork, potatoes, and fresh vegetables. Every time I open the swinging doorway, I feel a rush of adrenaline; rebelling against Mutti is always a thrill, and the punishment never takes that away. Thankfully, I know she isn't in here, so I rush inside before I'm seen.

"Good evening, Miss Inge," Marcel says as he removes his white chef hat. "I was just about to close the kitchen for the night, but what may I assist you with?"

I wander over to the butcher's block where he has folded the remaining slices of pork into parcel paper for storage in the cold box. Marcel was born and raised in Austria, just like I was. A little bit on the wider side, like me, he has a love for both eating and creating food, which is why he is such a good chef and friend. Marcel has been around for as long as I can remember, so I can't imagine what our apartment would be like without him, especially without the snacks he secretly gives to me.

I creep up in front of Marcel and paste a sugary-sweet smile on my face.

"Good evening, Marcel. I hope it's not too much of a bother, but I was wondering if you could possibly sneak me some of the delicacies you cooked up for the party. I could smell them from miles away, and it truly is too tempting to ignore."

Marcel frowns. Rolling his eyes, he wipes his greasy hands on his apron and takes it off. He looks tired as he sighs. "Now, now, Miss Inge. You know your mother's rules: no pork fat for you under any circumstances. I think she has made that very clear."

"Please, Marcel," I beg, clasping my hands together. "I would do anything to have just a little piece." My green eyes widen as I plead. "I have been dreaming about the way the flavorful fat melts in my mouth, the way the pork melts into the fresh bread, the way the salt complements the savory meat. It tastes like something too good to be on earth. Even a small bite of your brilliant creation would be sufficient."

Marcel's brown eyes search the door, and his bald head twitches with uncertainty. "You have no idea how much trouble I could be in with your mother if I allow you to have this." I start to whimper, and he holds up his hand. "But I don't have the time to sit and argue with you tonight because I know you will win, so to speed up the process, I will give you a little piece. But remember, this is just between us."

Marcel rinses his hands at the sink, pulls down a plate, and serves my delicious snack. I see a sprinkle of salt glistening on top of the black bread that is topped with three pieces of perfectly aligned pork fat. My mouth starts to water, and everything about this dish makes me forget about my desire for my mother's approval.

. . .

Inge climbed into the sagging bed.

"Goodnight, sweetheart," said Anna, wrapping her arms around her granddaughter.

"Goodnight, Omi," Inge replied, and warmth filled her cold heart as she fell asleep, comforted and content by her grandmother's side. Dreams of being reunited with her mother, however, haunted her restless sleep. She awoke early and shivering the next morning, clutching her threadbare blanket to her cold frame and wishing that these dreams would come true some day.

22 SEPTEMBER 7TH, 1941

BUXIÈRES-LES-MINES, FRANCE

The autumn breeze accelerated the speed of Inge's rusted second-hand bicycle, and she was nearly thrown to the ground after wobbling out of a pothole. However, the drag of her flat tires stabilized her. Anna always joked that she could predict when her granddaughter was arriving because the squealing of her tires could be heard from miles away. Inge continued to laugh at this joke to make her tired grandmother feel better, but it only added to her insecurity. She reminded herself that even though it was not her dream bicycle, being able to buy this one second-hand after weeks of hard work and saving was accomplishment enough.

Squeaking to a stop outside the butcher's shop, Inge was shocked to see a line snaking around the block. She spotted her best friend, Jacqueline, at the rear of the line. "Do you know why the entire village is in line?" Inge whispered.

"During last night's announcements, the announcement man told us that the butcher finally got beef fat after two months. So the whole village showed up really early this morning. I've been waiting in line for an hour already!" Jacqueline huffed and rolled her eyes, and the girls giggled. They had become best friends almost instantly when they were introduced by their grandmothers in June. Jacqueline had been staying with her grandparents during the summer.

"Are you serious, or is this a joke?"

"Would I joke about beef fat?" exclaimed Jacqueline, and they giggled again.

Inge felt such relief. Beef fat was a rare commodity, nowhere to be found, and her household had run out of their homemade tallow soap three weeks ago. She would be grateful to wash the dirt and dust from her body and hair with more than just water.

"I better get in line for some of this treasure before the butcher runs out!" she yelled to her friend, parking her bicycle and running to the end of the zigzagging queue.

During the first hour of waiting, Inge went over the list of groceries that her client, Mrs. Monnier, had given her: beef fat (if available), potatoes, and four slices of bread. During the next hour, she made a plan for obtaining her client's food: she would go to the general store after she got the beef fat because she could not afford to lose her place in line. Eventually, after an agonizing five-hour wait, she made it inside the shop.

"Next customer!" called the butcher from behind his wooden butcher's block.

Finally at the front of the line, Inge skipped up to the butcher. "May I please have two slices of beef fat?"

The butcher violently chopped at the meat, then handed the two slices to her. "Will that be all for today?

Nodding, Inge fished out almost all of the money she had earned that week to pay for her and Anna's slice. She then paid for the second slice separately, using the money she had been given by Mrs. Monnier.

"Thank you so much!" she shouted over her shoulder, running to her bicycle. The sunset surprised her. When she had arrived, it was early afternoon; now, nightfall was near. Shaking her head, she raced to the empty general store—she still had five minutes before it closed.

As she stepped inside, the welcome bell chimed. The three long shelves inside the store were nearly empty, except for a few broken chunks of bread. Frightened that their limited supply of farm goods had run out for the day, she rushed to the vegetable area in the far-left corner; if she did not deliver all of the requested goods, Mrs. Monnier would not pay her, and Inge needed that money to help Omi put food on the table. Rounding the shelf, she came upon a stack of potatoes and exhaled with relief. She rummaged to the bottom of the stack, knowing after so many errands that those potatoes would have the least amount of bruising. She chose five firm potatoes, and then ran to the shelves and collected four pieces of bread.

"Welcome Inge, what can I do for you today?" said the cashier.

"Hello! I would like to buy these potatoes and these slices of bread, please," she responded, pushing Mrs. Monnier's food toward the man.

After quickly paying, she stashed the goods in her bicycle's fraying straw basket and pointed her handlebars west.

Crossing an imaginary border, the scenery shifted from small, dilapidated shanties to crisply painted and sturdily built single-story houses. Instead of shoeless children with unruly hair running in the street, Inge saw well-dressed children with glossy golden curls careening down the streets on their shiny, polished bicycles, peddling with their wooden shoes. She envied them.

She dreamed of being one of those girls, but instead, she was stuck with unkempt red curls and fabric flats with soles that tore a little more each day. She was not unappreciative like they were, although she had been not very long ago. Now, Inge was a girl who worked to provide for herself and her grandmother, and she worried if they would have enough food to eat something for dinner each night. Inge had been forced to accept that even though she used to be one of those girls in Austria, she was a totally different child in Buxières-les-Mines.

She resumed pedaling down the muddy road, her long auburn strands flying in the wind. The cool breeze she felt against her cheeks freed her from reality. She imagined being in a small town outside New York City, riding toward her apartment where she lived with Mutti and Omi. This daydream was something that she had allowed herself ever since their arrival in the village. She imagined that they lived in a four-bedroom apartment, decorated by Stella's sculptures and paintings, just like in Vienna. Their living room would overlook a beautiful park filled with colorful flowers and healthy, green trees. Marcel would slip her pork fat during Stella's parties with live music, and Maria would get on Inge's nerves about minding her manners and presenting herself correctly.

Inge arrived outside her employer's two-bedroom home. The bright beige house sat on a perfectly manicured lawn beside a small plot of red poppy flowers. Inge walked up the concrete steps, rang the doorbell, and stepped back onto the grass, per Mrs. Monnier's instructions. "Good afternoon, Mrs. Monnier. I came to drop off your groceries."

"Which you should have dropped off four hours ago!" clucked Mrs. Monnier, persing her bright red lips.

"But I was able to get you all of the items on your list today," Inge nervously explained. "The butcher finally received beef fat!"

"Well, that is what I hired you to do, isn't it?" said Mrs. Monnier.

Inge looked at the ground and choked out a faint, "Yes, Madame."

"Girl!" yelled Mrs. Monnier. "Look at me when I speak to you! Leave the packages on the doorstep. I have important things to do." Mrs. Monnier's eyes flashed the same blue as the flowers on her dress. Inge placed the package on the doorstep while Mrs. Monnier backed away, clutching her wallet close to her body. She then took out some money, but only after Inge had returned to the bottom step.

"I'm surprised at how someone like you living on the other side of the village could complete this task. Your people are usually too lazy or too simple-minded. But you are a good girl," praised Mrs. Monnier as if she were talking to a dog. She then quickly placed the money on the ground in front of Inge's feet so that she would not catch the vermin she believed infested most of the poor.

"Thank you, Madame," said Inge, inwardly smarting at the disgraceful treatment.

Mrs. Monnier backed into her house, shooing Inge away with the flick of her hand.

Getting back onto her red bike, Inge felt defeated. She knew she was no longer as well off as Mrs. Monnier, but that gave her no right to treat Inge any differently than she would her friends' children just because they dressed, worked, and lived in contrasting ways. The way she spoke to Inge in a babyish tone was infuriating. None of Inge's employers allowed her into their houses because they believed she would steal from them. Being branded as a thief was humiliating, and Inge felt less than human. It hurt to be treated this way, so she could only hope that all of this was temporary and that her life would someday be back to normal.

23 JANUARY 13TH, 1942

BUXIÈRES-LES-MINES, FRANCE

Knocking harder on the door of the farmhouse the second time, Inge wondered why Mrs. Rosier was not answering. "Mrs. Rosier?" she called. "Are you there? I have a letter for Jacqueline, and I brought your butter ration."

Inge had been riding groceries over to her friend's grandparents for the past few months since Jacqueline had returned home after her summer visit. Jacqueline's village was 22 kilometers from Buxières-les-Mines, so the best friends had not seen each other since school began in September. But they had written letters back and forth every week, and Jacqueline's grandmother had been happy to post for Inge.

"Mrs. Rosier?" she tried again, then peered into a dusty window on the porch, knowing that Anna would be ashamed of her impoliteness.

Inge jumped as she heard the wooden door spring open and saw the pink bald head of Mr. Rosier peek around it.

"Ahhh, Inge," he said. "It is not a good time."

"I'm sorry," said Inge. "I will leave. I was just bringing your rations and a letter for Jacqueline."

He winced at the sound of his granddaughter's name and brought his hand to his brow.

"What is it, Mr. Rosier?"

Clearing his throat, he hesitated, then took a deep breath. "Inge, my dear, our family has been lost. There were bombings in their village. They were killed in their beds."

Inge blinked. She must have misheard. "They were all killed by a bombing? Even Jacqueline?"

Mr. Rosier nodded as tears streamed from his eyes. "My son and his wife and their children." He began to sob, and turned back into the house.

How could it be true? She had just read Jacqueline's latest letter two days ago and could hear her best friend's laughter through her written words. *I know you have a crush on Claude LeClerc,* she had teased.

Inge wandered off the porch, remembering how mad she had been at Jacqueline's insinuation, and then she stopped, sinking to her knees and pounding the frozen ground with her fists. "No!" she cried. "No, no, no! It's not fair!" she screamed as an icy emptiness filled her heart once again.

"I'm home," Inge called, opening the hotel room door late that evening. She could not bear sharing the news of Jacqueline's death with her grandmother, so she had returned to school to clean the chalkboards for Monsieur Dubois, and then asked to run extra errands for Madame Gaudet.

Stepping inside, Inge gasped at the sight of an unexpected guest. "Uncle Manny!" she cried and ran into his arms, remembering his familiar smell and the prickle of his woolen sweater on her cheek. She began to weep.

"Oh, Inge, I've missed you too!" Emanuel patted her back. "It's okay, don't cry. I'm here now!"

Inge hugged him tightly for several more seconds and then dried her eyes with her sleeves. "I'm sorry, I'm just so happy to see you. How have you been? Tell me all about your time in the Foreign Legion. Did you have lots of adventures?"

"Well, instead of working in combat, I was sent to build railroads, which I now understand inside and out. But then I got sick with malaria, so they sent me back home to you."

"Oh, Uncle Manny, I'm so sorry. That must have been awful. Are you feeling better?"

"Yes, my dear, don't worry. I made a full recovery, and I feel great now that I am back with you and Omi."

Anna's soft mouth curved into a cautious smile. "Inge, we have exciting news to share!" she began. "Your uncle will be working as a painter here in the village! And we have a surprise for you. Let's go!"

Inge noticed that Anna had packed up their suitcases. As Emanuel grabbed them, she took Anna's hand, and they left the room.

The trio walked only a block down the main street before turning onto a smaller side street. Minutes later, they came upon a line of one-room dwellings made of scavenged, uneven pieces of tin and wood.

Inge tilted her head and looked at Anna.

"Thanks to your and Emanuel's hard work, we have enough money to rent our very own home!"

Inge felt disappointed, her stomach suddenly souring. "Oh, I..." she faltered, not finding the words. Instead, she forced a bright, appreciative smile.

"We can move right in!" insisted Emanuel, handing Inge her suitcase.

He pushed open the ill-fitting door, and Inge stepped inside. The dirt floor was cold underneath her feet, and the temperature seemed lower inside the shack. A small, two-person table lined one wall and held a soot-stained alcohol burner; a tiny bed had been pushed into the opposite corner.

"What do you think of our new home, my dear?" asked Anna nervously, sensing her granddaughter's hesitation.

"It's great, Omi! I'm just so happy that we will all be together again."

"Well, there are a few things that you should know. Unfortunately, there is no electricity, and if you need to use the bathroom, you must use the hole behind the shed. We will not be able to purchase toilet paper, so you must use leaves."

"Okay," Inge whispered, biting her lip to conceal her despair.

"Well, everyone must be tired," said Emanuel, "and I set up the bed earlier today, so why don't we all get some rest? We can unpack tomorrow."

Closing her heavy eyes, Inge nodded, and the three arranged themselves onto the creaking bed. Inge trembled under their thin, ragged blanket, hearing the cold wind whistle through the cracks in the walls of the shack. Once she was certain the adults were fast asleep, she doubled the blanket onto Anna and sank down onto the floor in the opposite corner of the room, feeling the splintered wood pierce her back. Looking up, she realized that she could peer out at the stars through the large holes in the roof. Inge buried her face into her knees and wept for all of her losses. She had pledged to put on a brave face for her family, but for now, she would allow herself to feel all of the sadness and longing that she had been holding back for hours.

24 MAY 21ST, 1942

BUXIÈRES-LES-MINES, FRANCE

Inge had borne the nickname *la pore Inge* for the entire school year because Anna had refused to let her spend time with her friends until she finished working and completing her schoolwork for the day. However, as she approached the school for what could possibly be the last time, she silently thanked her grandmother, recognizing that her sacrifices were now paying off.

Pushing open the door, Inge's eyes instantly fell on the gnarled log used to prop up the front table after Renée had tripped over the broken leg, and she smiled. Looking around the schoolhouse, she realized that the few hours she had spent in that room each day were the only moments she spent not worrying about money or work. She brushed her callused fingers along the uneven wooden desk and wondered if she would ever have a carefree space like this again.

As she approached Monsieur Dubois' desk, the floorboard beneath her left foot creaked, and she smiled again, remembering the older kids trying to sneak into class late, with this same wood board repeatedly giving them away.

"Ah, Inge," he greeted her. "Are you ready for your exit exam?"

"Absolutely!"

Most children felt nervous around the stoic, cold-hearted teacher, but Inge had promised herself on the first day of school that she would end up on his good side. She applied herself to her studies and ran errands for Monsieur Dubois after school, which allowed her to escape his sharp tongue and cruel punishments—and make money while doing it.

"Take a seat, and let's get started." Monsieur Dubois handed her a weathered exam sheet with lead smudges staining the script. He explained the instructions and told her that he was certain she would have no problems and complete the exam in a short time.

The three-section test covered Inge's favorite subjects: math, French, and history. Just as Monsieur Dubois had predicted, she finished quickly and easily. Shaking out her lead-stained right hand, she hurried to her teacher's desk and placed the exam before him, confident that today would, in fact, be her last day of school ever.

"Mmhmmm," began Monsieur Dubois as he graded her results, moving his pen from one answer to the next. She watched his eyes travel along each line of writing, and began to feel uncertain.

"Inge," he paused, and her stomach flipped. "You passed. And with excellence too!"

Overwhelmed, Inge stood frozen. Then she squeaked, "I passed?"

Monsieur Dubois nodded. "You have proven to be wise beyond your years," he said, chuckling. His intense gaze relaxed. "Graduating two years early is quite an accomplishment."

"Thank you for everything, Monsieur Dubois!" Inge was beaming. "I learned so much as your student. Until we meet again!"

"Omi!" Inge exclaimed, tripping through the front door.

"Yes, dear?" she answered from the bed and slowly sat up.

Inge gasped for air before continuing, winded after running all the way from school. "I passed the graduation test this morning!"

Anna's frail face lit up. "My goodness! You continue to make me prouder and prouder each day. Congratulations!"

"Thank you, Omi, I want to make you proud, and now that I am old enough, there is something I want to ask you," Inge replied in a more serious tone, standing up taller and straighter.

"Go on..." Anna responded.

"From now on, I would like to be called Monique."

"Monique? But why?"

"When we spoke German in Austria, everyone pronounced my name correctly, but here, the French pronounce the *I* in Inge like an *A*, and it sounds like their word for *monkey*. I already look like a monkey with my unruly hair and freckles, so having Inge as a name makes it worse." Tears formed in her eyes as she continued. "Monique is also a French name, so I would fit in more if I went by it, especially since it seems like we are going to be living here for a while."

"My darling, you know better than to listen to them! Inge is a beautiful name for a beautiful girl, regardless of its pronunciation or origin. What would Mutti think?" Grasping Inge's sweaty hand and looking into her worried eyes, Anna took a few moments of contemplation before continuing. "I suppose this must be important to you given that today is the first time I can remember that you have asked me for anything."

Inge nodded.

"And I guess it won't hurt for you to have a fresh start. Not to mention that you truly deserve something special, as I know how hard you have been working to provide for us since our arrival here..." Anna smiled tenderly. "Well... I suppose your new name is Monique."

"Really? I'm Monique? It's all right with you? Thank you so much, Omi, you truly are wonderful!" Inge exuberantly hugged her grandmother's small frame, feeling Anna's delicate bones beneath her hands.

"But you will always be Inge to me, Monique," Anna softly whispered into her granddaughter's ear.

25 APRIL 20TH, 1943

BUXIÈRES-LES-MINES, FRANCE

In a dwelling not far away from the Kupfer's, a young boy named Thomas—Monique's former classmate—lay awake between his parents on a horsehair mattress, the rumbling of his stomach making deep sleep impossible.

Suddenly, a furious pounding at the door startled his family awake.

"Thomas!" His mother, Sarah whispered his name, then bolted from the bed and quietly opened the wooden door of a large armoire that she had inherited from her grandfather—the only remaining furniture from their large apartment in Lyons.

"Is it happening?" whimpered Thomas as he followed his mother and father into the wardrobe. It was the moment they had dreaded since they moved to this village. Unease slithered down Thomas's spine as he crawled across the smooth wood.

The Goldbergs had practiced this scenario many times, but it had not prepared them for the real event, and their ragged breathing revealed their terror. They entered the closet in which they hid had a false back, concealed with sheets and drapery. They had to stand somewhat overlapping each other in order to all fit inside the compartment, but it was the only thing that could possibly protect them from the Nazis.

Thomas's small body melted into his mother's, and he wished he could be invisible, like *The Shadow*, a hero in the American comic book his parents had given him for his birthday two years before. A scene in which his father and mother were beaten by the Nazi guards played repeatedly in his mind, and he began to bite his nails.

"Open up!" yelled an angry voice with a thick German accent.

Thomas could hear the slap of a whip against the door. The silence that followed comforted him, but seconds later, a loud thud shook the wardrobe as the men kicked the shack door to the ground.

Sarah gasped, terrified, and immediately pressed her lips into a firm line. Instinctively reaching for Thomas, she squeezed his frail hand.

Thomas could just make out the intruders through a knot in the wall of the armoire. The three men wore stiff green coats with multicolored patches across their arms and chests; Thomas' gaze rested on the one that mattered most: the swastika on their armbands. In the middle of each of their white collars was a small, gold crucifix, and behind each of their backs rested a large black gun.

The Nazis stormed into the Goldberg's home, the bouncing beams of their flashlights illuminating every corner.

"Where are these *Untermenschen*?" shouted one of the officers, spitting onto the floor, which was now covered in wood chips.

"They could be hiding out back. You check there, and you search that wardrobe," one of the men instructed, pointing the others toward each destination. "Let's make those Jewish vermin regret the day they were born!" he screamed.

In the small, dark closet, Thomas snuggled close to his mother and father, clutching their hands as tightly as he could. Frozen like a statue, he refused to believe that the nightmare he feared most had actually become a reality.

The Goldberg's held a collective breath as the Nazis' boots banged on the floor of their shack. As they edged closer to the closet,

Thomas' fear turned to terror, and he could feel the wetness of his mother's tears against his cheek. He knew that this was the end.

The false wall of the armoire wrenched open, and the evil glare of the Nazi soldiers met the terrified look of the Goldbergs.

The two men were chuckling. "Get out, you disobedient rats! You really thought that you could hide from us?"

In fear of their lives, Sarah, Asher, and Thomas did as they were told, exchanging sorrowful looks. Thomas's breath grew labored when his mother mouthed that she loved him as he stared into her fearful eyes. They knew what would happen next.

Each family member was handcuffed by a different Nazi, and they were dragged out of the one room that had kept them safe. Before leaving, one of the Nazis pointed his flashlight into the dark closet. He grinned when the light hit upon the small stash of money, jewelry, and identification papers that the Goldbergs had been hiding. "This is your repayment for existing," he shouted. "Disgusting animals!"

Tears trailed down Thomas's face. He no longer felt like a boy or even a human. The Germans were treating him like the dirt under their boots.

Sarah and Asher shared a panicked look as their son was pulled away. With their sorrow-filled eyes, they believed that they had failed as parents for not being able to protect their son from the horrors of the Nazis.

The following evening, Emanuel rushed home after work to share the terrible news of the Goldbergs' arrest. He had secretly joined the *Forces Françaises de l'Intérieur,* one of France's underground resistance groups rebelling against the Nazi occupation. He always had the latest news about attacks in their village and the surrounding areas.

"Mutti! Monique!" cried Emanuel, bursting through the door. "I have very sad news."

Monique and Anna shared a puzzled look. "What is it, Uncle Manny?" asked Monique.

"Do you remember our neighbors, the Goldbergs?"

Monique nodded. Of course she remembered the Goldbergs. How could she ever forget the peculiar boy from school?

"They were taken away last night," Emanuel said. "Someone found out that they were Jewish and told the Nazis." His eyes darted from left to right, as if in fear that someone unseen was listening in.

Anna covered her mouth with her hands. "When something like this happens so close to home it—"

"I know, Mutti, I know," Emanuel whispered to Anna, who shook her head and closed her eyes. He knew that Anna was contemplating *their* safety.

"Poor Thomas," Monique added. She only understood a little bit of what was going on, but she knew one thing for certain: Thomas and his family were Jewish, and the officers in the village did not like people who fell under that category, so they took them away.

Suddenly, Monique realized that the reason Thomas was always so peculiar and nervous was because he was afraid for his life. Now she understood and felt deep sorrow for his fear and what his family had experienced.

She would have been frightened for her family as well, if she had known about her true heritage. However, she had been kept ignorant of her family history her whole life. Neither she nor anyone else in her village had the slightest clue that she was Jewish.

26 AUGUST 5TH, 1943

BUXIÈRES-LES-MINES, FRANCE

With rations decreasing each week, fending off starvation became the priority for the villagers. Their constant pangs of hunger rendered them oblivious to the fact that there were Jews hiding amongst them. Monique continued to take work anywhere she could while Anna grew frailer at an alarming rate without a proper diet and no access to medicine.

Emanuel continued his work in the French Resistance. In order to avoid detection, his group never met at the same location and only carried out their work a distance from Buxières-les-Mines. Today, they were meeting in a picturesque field 20 kilometers outside the village, where few soldiers ever patrolled the quiet road.

Emanuel had borrowed Monique's bike for the meeting. After hiding it in the long grass of the field, he approached the group.

"Good morning, Robinson," said Alphonse, the leader, greeting Emanuel by his pseudonym. Alphonse had been a member of *Forces Françaises de l'Intérieur* since its inception. Older but still strong, Alphonse towered over the rest of the group. He ran his fingers through his salt-and-pepper hair and bit down on the blunt pencil that he held between his teeth, checking over the assignments for the day.

Emanuel gave him a curt nod, signaling his readiness, and Alphonse nodded back in reply. "Today," he said, "we make our stand."

The men exchanged anxious glances. They had not been told of the date or the details of their latest operation, for the sake of secrecy.

"We'll be ambushing the Germans at the railroad tracks in Souvigny. One group will disassemble the railroad tracks, and one will disable the train engine."

Usually dour and serious, the men now wore wide smiles and patted one another on the back with congratulations. They rarely got to see any action and never got this close to the Nazis, so the prospect of making a real change was exciting.

With no formal uniform, the resistance usually wore whatever they could find for their missions. Most remained in their civilian clothing: thin, patched coats and threadbare wool pants. Their haphazard appearance helped camouflage them—after all, who would believe that these tired, hungry villagers were an effective, well-organized fighting force?

"We have planned this very carefully. I have watched this site for the past month, and every Thursday evening at five o'clock, the Nazis leave the train for two hours. They take a bus somewhere, probably to feast on our stolen food, and return two hours later. During this time, the train is left unguarded."

This mission was personal for many in the group, especially Emanuel. His former wife had been persuaded by her boss to join the Nazi Party in 1938, which eventually corrupted her love for her husband and her country. Ever since then, he had vowed to do what he could to put a stop to the Nazi rule.

The train tracks next to the men started to rumble, and the group quickly began walking toward the billowing smoke high above the trees. It was time to commence their work.

Hiding within the thick forest flanking the station, the men watched the Nazis disembark, laughing and talking raucously amongst themselves. Emanuel felt his stomach sour, disgusted that people who carried out such cruel and unimaginable deeds could act so carefree.

Pointing at the empty train, Alphonse signaled it was time to get started. He had appointed Emanuel the leader of the railroad group and given him one of the group's two guns. Weapons were hard to come by and too expensive to purchase for every group member, so Emanuel had taken it with pride and pledged to protect them.

From their place of hiding, the men ran toward the train, half of them aiming to damage the train's engine and the other half to disassemble the tracks.

Working frantically, Emanuel's group removed the wooden slats of the track using hammers and crowbars. In a short amount of time, the men's arms ached, their throats were dry, and their legs were starting to buckle from squatting down. They pushed the pain away as they remembered their destroyed homes and their stolen property. Some had lost loved ones in the occupation, and they channeled their hatred into their work.

"We can move on to the outer rail now!" signaled Hubert, one of Emanuel's group members, as he removed the last piece of wood on the tracks.

Working together, they heaved upward with their crowbars, lifting and bending the steel rail.

"Well done, everyone!" exclaimed Emanuel, wiping the sweat off of his face. "We should get back to the rendezvous point."

As they moved toward the station, figures appeared in the distance. Emanuel raised his hand to stop his men. Squinting into the dusky horizon, he attempted to distinguish whether the figures were uniformed. As they materialized, Emanuel's heart jumped when he realized that the figures were all in green. They had not discussed how to proceed if the Nazis came back to the station early, and the men looked expectantly at their leader, terror shining in their eyes. Their crowbars would be no match for rifles and revolvers.

Before they could escape or alert the group still inside the train, seven Nazi officers exited the station and came face-to-face with Emanuel's group. Noting the hammers and crowbars, their suspicious gazes turned to the torn-up tracks from which the men had just come. Enraged, one of them yelled, "Ambush!"

The Nazis came at Emanuel and his men, who began to sprint toward the cover of the forest. Emanuel's arms were pumping, and his chest was pleading for air. His exhausted legs were threatening to give out, but still he ran.

The sound of gunshots pierced Emanuel's ears, and he ducked. Ahead of him, Hubert fell, and Emanuel stopped instantly. Instinct and loyalty told him to try to save his comrade.

Another gunshot sounded, and Emanuel was plunged forward onto the ground. He felt a searing heat in his chest. Peering down, he saw his white shirt beginning to fill with blood. His blood. Gasping for air, Emanuel pleaded for help, but the last thing he saw before his vision went dark was the smug face of the man who had shot him.

27 SEPTEMBER 19TH, 1943

BUXIÈRES-LES-MINES, FRANCE

As Monique ran errands for clients or worked her shifts at the local hotel's cinema, her eyes instinctively searched her surroundings, hoping to find her uncle standing on a street corner, or in line at the general store. Each day without word from Emanuel brought more uncertainty. From her mother, letters and small gifts would occasionally arrive, informing them that she was well. But it had been well over a month since the day Emanuel left to paint houses and never returned. Monique needed him to be safe. She did not know how much more loss she or her grandmother could take.

One evening, as Monique sat at the table waiting for supper and Anna slowly stirred their turnip soup, they were startled by a short rap at the door. Nerves taut, Anna yelped in surprise, knocking the rusted pot off the alcohol burner.

"Don't worry, Omi! I'll clean it up!" Monique cried as she grabbed a ragged cloth from the wash basin to sop up the spill. "Were you hurt?"

Anna shook her head and ambled to the door. No one had ever knocked on their door at such a late hour, and for the briefest moment, Monique allowed herself to believe that it would be her mother.

Anna pulled open the door to reveal a gaunt, stoic man standing on the porch, holding his hat. He hesitated and bit his lip, and then began to speak. "My apologies for interrupting you at such a late hour. My name is Alphonse, and it's a pleasure to finally meet you. I worked with Emanuel Kupfer."

Monique gasped and approached the door. "You did? We have been looking for him for over a month!"

The man stared at her.

"Won't you please come in?" asked Anna. "I am Emanuel's mother, Anna, and this is my granddaughter, Monique."

Alphonse nodded, "Actually, ma'am, would you mind if we spoke alone?"

Anna's eyes filled with dread, and she reached out for Monique's hand, shaking her head.

Alphonse stepped inside, and began again, sighing. "I am not sure if either of you were aware, but Emanuel was a member of the Resistance." He waited for a reaction and continued when both women raised their eyebrows. "It was necessary for him to keep it from you so that you would be safe in case he was compromised. Unfortunately, one of our operations was discovered by the Nazis last month, and..." He swallowed.

Anna whimpered, and Monique felt her lean more heavily onto her arm.

Looking away, Alphonse whispered, "Your son acted so courageously. He was trying to save the lives of his comrades, but it wasn't enough. We just didn't have enough guns to protect them. The Nazis, they... they shot him... in the heart." He choked out the last words.

Monique's hand flew to her mouth. She could not believe his words.

"Is... is he alive?"

"I'm very sorry," said Alphonse. "He didn't make it. He died quickly."

Monique held her breath for a moment, then she broke into wrenching sobs.

"No, no," Anna wailed, sinking to the floor beside her. "My sweet, sweet boy."

"I want you to know how much he loved you and his country. He was a hero for France, and we will be offering both of you French citizenship in honor of his sacrifice. Emanuel was a brave soldier and a loyal friend. My deepest condolences to you." Alphonse bowed and let himself out of the shack.

Monique huddled over her grandmother, wrapping her arms around her, burying her face in Anna's hair. She felt Anna's body heave with each sob, and Monique knew that she could not succumb to her own grief. She lifted her grandmother from the floor and carried her to the bed, covering her with the blanket and stroking her damp hair back from her cheeks. The pair huddled together until their breathing slowed. Monique knew that she needed to be strong for Anna now, to keep the weight of this grief from crushing her grandmother.

28 JANUARY 2ND, 1944

BUXIÈRES-LES-MINES, FRANCE

After learning of Emanuel's death, Anna became lifeless, growing weaker and more inward each day. Her skin grayed, and deep cracks ran down her thin chapped lips. When she opened her eyes each morning, she was overcome by a cascade of fresh guilt, plagued with thoughts of what she could have done differently to save her son.

Unable to get out of bed, the roles in the house had reversed. Monique became the caregiver to the fragile, deteriorating woman. She cooked the meals and earned the money to keep them fed. Each morning, she looked into Anna's glassy eyes for hints of her grandmother's vitality, fearing that it might never return.

On Monique's special day, she roused her grandmother and sponged her face and neck with a torn cloth.

"Where are we going?" asked Anna, confused. She had forgotten many small details lately, worrying her granddaughter. But the arrangements for that day had been made months earlier by Anna and Father Belmont, the local priest; Anna secretly wanted Monique to be involved with the Church to further conceal her Jewish identity.

"It's a surprise, Omi," Monique replied, smoothing down her wispy hair and helping her to the side of the bed.

Monique had dressed herself in the best of their donated clothing for the day's event. Studying her appearance in the small, cracked mirror, she realized that she was becoming an adult far too quickly. Inside, she still felt like a girl seeking her mother's approval. She glanced at her grandmother hunched over on the side of the bed and shook herself of her doubt. Monique was determined to get her grandmother out of the house today. It would not only be spiritually therapeutic for Anna, but it would also force her to walk again.

Unable to discern whether or not Anna had even heard her words, Monique helped her into her coat and led her outside for the first time since Emanuel's death. They shuffled down the almost empty main street at a slow speed, the cool morning breeze brushing lightly against their skin. The added weight of Anna made walking nearly unbearable for Monique, her feet blistering in ragged shoes.

The pair finally approached the large church at the center of the village, its bells signaling that the hour for worship and praise had begun. As the deep chimes intensified, Monique's heart rate quickened. She turned up the walk to the church, helping her grandmother up the stone steps and leading her through the welcoming doors of Église Saint Maurice. Although the wooden interior lacked the elaborate stained-glass and intricate sculptures of St. Stephens, this church was energized by the attendance of almost every villager of Buxières-les-Mines. Monique and Anna carefully made their way down the center aisle to the front row. Monique would take her First Holy Communion today, and she sat at the end of the pew, ready to be called up.

The congregation quieted when Father Belmont entered, adjusting his white robe as he approached the nave. He bowed and kissed the altar, then welcomed the villagers to Sunday Mass. Monique felt her nerves well up with each passing minute. As the priest finally took communion for himself and began to genuflect, she knew it would be soon.

"I would like to call up all of the children who have decided to confirm their belief in the Catholic Church today, *la première communion.*"

Monique felt the light pressure of Anna's hand on her leg and lifted herself slowly from the wooden pew. Looking over, she saw her grandmother's reassuring smile, which gave her the encouragement she needed to join the procession of children to the altar.

Monique towered over even the oldest child in the line, having joined the church community at such an older age. Although she had felt awkward and out of place in the months leading up to her communion, the members of the church had made her feel extremely welcome following her uncle's death. They had contributed every piece of clothing on her body that day, even sewing her a new white dress for the special ceremony.

Watching each child approach and halt before the priest, she tried to concentrate on her connection to God, but all she could think about was the lottery ticket that Renée had given her as a congratulatory gift and she had misplaced.

At her turn, Monique beamed proudly as she approached Father Belmont and received the small piece of bread he held out to her. "The Body of Christ."

"Amen," Monique replied, and Father Belmont pressed the host onto her tongue, then placed his hand gently on the top of her head while blessing her with a final prayer.

As she returned to her seat to pray, Monique tried to overcome her excitement and keep her focus on the ceremony, and as she peeked through half-closed lids at the congregants in front of her, she saw a small sea of smiling, friendly faces meeting her gaze. She was filled with pride as she met Anna's smiling eyes, her grandmother's face flush with color for the first time since her uncle's death. Monique returned to her pew to pray, her heart full, yet something was missing. A small part of Monique ached for her mother and uncle to have been there, to witness her First Communion.

29 JUNE 24TH, 1944

BUXIÈRES-LES-MINES, FRANCE

Monique stiffly pushed open the back door of the farmhouse, grabbing an empty metal bucket off the back porch. Although it was not yet dawn, her feet found the long path through the front field, leading her to the road as they had each day for the past two months on her daily quest for water. She trudged down the dirt-paved road that led to Buxières-les-Mines, distracted by green trees and the morning songbirds barely visible against the brightening sky. The nightingale's melodies were a pleasant diversion from the inescapable fatigue weighing down upon her. With each passing day, her gait grew slower, and it took more effort to carry the full bucket back to the Nadeau farm from town. She knew that today the grueling kilometer back to the farm would seem indomitable.

Monique's fingers were swollen and purple at the tips by the time her pinching loafers finally turned back onto the dewy front pasture. Her knuckles burned from the weight of the water, and her arm began to tremble, splashing precious droplets of clean water onto the ground. She could see the roof of the farmhouse peeking out over the rolling fields, willing her to take another step toward it like each day before. If she stopped, Monique knew that she would not go on and would lose her job. Then she and her grandmother would starve.

The memory of her mother's most recent package brought slight relief from her pain. She could suddenly smell the fresh coffee beans and feel the silk lining of the majestic cobalt coat against her aching arm. It had become a surrogate for her mother's touch, so although she had immediately sold the coffee beans for the equivalent of two week's wages, she kept the coat. Since it was too expensive to obtain materials for correspondence, Monique had not yet thanked her mother for the luxurious gift, but she dreamed of the day when they would be reunited in America, and she watched and waited for the letter that would include the necessary passports for her and Anna.

She finally reached the door of the house and entered, heaving the bucket onto the cupboard with the last of her strength.

Nathan Nadeau was already sitting at the kitchen table. "Good morning!" he chirped brightly, looking up from his breakfast. "Sit down, please. Rest a moment."

Monique smiled and noticed how the rising sun glinted in Nathan's kind brown eyes. "Thank you, Nathan."

He rose from his chair, gathering his plate and fork, as she sat down. Nathan had finished every last bite of his small portion of the breakfast available for the family, but she recognized the faint yellow stain of an egg yolk. Although Monique was used to going without, she still felt the burn of envy heat her face. That meager meal was more than Nathan gave her and Anna to eat in an entire day.

"Good to see you this morning, Monique," Nathan said, reaching for his soft worn hat hanging beside the door. "I will be in the barn if you need me. Please get the cows into the back pasture as soon as possible." He nodded his goodbye, pulling at his gaping trousers and exposing his cracked black gum boots. Even Nathan, whose farm had one of the most successful harvests in the region, looked like a peasant. The Germans were taking everything.

"I'll get started on it right after I make breakfast for the children," she assured him, as she stood slowly, and began rooting around for her apron in a rusted drawer.

The farmhouse boasted a bright kitchen, so Monique did not mind starting the day there. She whipped together two of the only remaining hen's eggs and placed two strips of bacon on a skillet on the pot belly stove. Salivating over the delicacy, she allowed herself to remember the sweetness of the meat and the saltiness of the fat. *How long had it been?* she mused and wondered how her old friend Marcel had fared through the war. *Was it possible that he was still in Vienna?* She returned her attention to the stove when she heard the bacon begin to pop; daydreaming was dangerous when food was so scarce and there was work to be done.

After making breakfast and cleaning the kitchen, Monique was forced to confront the single hardest chore she had on the farm: herding the cows. Cursed with bovinophobia, she loathed the task, but knew that it was extremely lucky to have any milk at all. Nathan still owned at least six dairy cows, even with passing German soldiers carting off any number they wished.

Stepping onto the back porch, Monique's voice broke into the quiet morning, "Alfie, where are you? Alfie! It's time to herd the cows!"

Stillness echoed.

"Alfie! Alfie!" she called again and walked toward the back pasture's fence where she believed the border collie would be waiting.

The yard was empty.

The dog's mischief always increased the amount of time she spent on this chore. She whistled but was again met with silence. Fatigue gripped her mind and body, and she fought back her frustration. She had to complete this task; disappointing Nathan could risk her job.

Looking back at the house, Monique spied a mop of gray wispy fur flattened onto the back porch like a rug. Laughing to herself, she shook her head. Alfie must have come up behind her from the front of the house. The dog always tried to outsmart her.

Monique yelled his name again in a high, friendly tone, attempting to coax him to her. She scoffed as he sprang up, sprinted back around the house, and disappeared into the front field. She was forced to follow. As her search continued, Monique's tone vacillated sharply between feigned sweetness and true spite. She ridiculed herself for not thinking to save just a nibble of the bacon from breakfast as a lure for Alfie.

Nearing the road, she heard the chatter of neighbors and recognized her old customer Monsieur Ribault and his son, Guy, who were leading a goat toward town.

"Old Alfie has bested you again, eh Monique?" the older man grinned.

Monique's cheeks burned bright as she heard Guy stifle a snort of laughter, and she grimaced at the young man.

"Don't you have somewhere to be?" she replied.

"Ah, Monique," Monsieur Ribault answered. "Please excuse our teasing. Laughter is so rare in these times." He pointed to the goat. "Our Bett has stopped making milk, so we must sell her in order to buy some for the younger children."

Monique instantly regretted her harsh tone and shook her head, waving goodbye. Still, she refused to continue the comedic show for any passersby, so she marched back toward the east field, deciding to herd the cows herself.

She lifted the latch on the fence and walked toward the herd, swallowing her apprehension. Approaching a small pack of heifers, she circled around them and started a slow jog in the direction of the back field. As she picked up speed, a few cows trailed her with their calves. One by one, a black and cream-colored parade formed behind Monique, and she could not suppress a smirk. *They think I am the Grand Marshal,* she thought, and began pumping her arm up and down to the beat of the big band playing in her head.

Once she closed the paddock on the back field, she counted the heads. There were only five. She counted again, this time taking notice of their distinctions. *The bull*, she thought, as she bit her lip. It had been a fleeting victory.

Anxiety bubbled at the thought of driving the bull alone. Monique started for the barn. *I must get Nathan,* she thought, admitting defeat. Just then, she heard the bull's loud grunting. He was close—close enough that she believed she could corral him alone.

Reopening the gate to the back pasture, Monique saw that the bull had started a slow gallop. She took a few steps toward him and realized that he was charging directly at her. As he picked up speed, she was entranced by his dark eyes. There were tiny crystalline drops of moisture on his snout as he huffed out heavy gusts of misty breath into the morning air. Monique suddenly recognized the danger of her position and sprinted toward the gate, hurling herself to the side just as she felt the bull's hot breath on the back of her neck. He bellowed loudly once inside the corral, announcing his dissatisfaction. Monique felt proud, even as she wiped the manure that she had fallen into from her hands and dress. Today *was* a victory.

30 AUGUST 25TH, 1944

BUXIÈRES-LES-MINES, FRANCE

Anna looked small and drained, hunched over her plate at the small wooden table in their room in the back of the Nadeau farmhouse. Rations were no longer reliable, and the remaining food had become extremely expensive, so Monique's meager earnings could not support them. They were relying on the charity of their neighbors to survive. Tonight, Nathan had shared a few potatoes. It could have felt like a dream come true for Anna, but she was having trouble forcing the dinner down.

Monique glanced at her grandmother with concern and shifted restlessly on the splintered chair. "Aren't you hungry, Omi?"

Anna looked up and met Monique's worried gaze. Her drooping, distant eyes were dull.

"How was your day?" asked Monique, hoping to wake her grandmother from her daze. Anna silently nodded and fixed her stare on the tomato garden outside their small window.

Noise on the road outside startled Monique. Wiping the dust from the window, she realized that it was 6 p.m., the time when the residents of the village gathered near the farms to hear the evening announcements. Owning a radio was a luxury no one in the countryside could afford.

Monique stood up, rushing to get her shoes. "Omi, it's time for the announcements," she said, grabbing her grandmother's cane.

Anna turned back to the table and bowed her head. "Monique, I just don't have the strength right now," she sighed, closing her eyes.

Monique's heart was heavy. She knew her grandmother's physical strength had begun to return, but the emotional scars from Emanuel's death were weighing upon her. She was losing her will to live. The last time she'd had the energy to even leave their room was months ago.

"Please come tonight, Omi. It's just outside," insisted Monique, wrapping a worn sweater around Anna's shoulders. "It's not a long walk." She knew the crowd and the crisp night air would offer her grandmother brief relief from her pain and was determined to convince her.

Sighing, Anna grasped the head of her cane with one hand and pushed out of the chair. She reached for Monique's arm, and they walked slowly out the door.

Beyond their cramped, stuffy room lay a barren field, then the road. The setting sun beamed against their skin as they made their way toward the gathering crowd. Noticing her grandmother breathe in the smell of the dewy flowers, Monique was relieved that she had convinced her to take in some fresh air.

They found an empty spot near the center of the chattering crowd. Farmers, still in their work hats and thin linen shirts, towered over their wives and children. Heads turned as the sound of an irregular drum beat signaled that the news of the day was inching nearer.

Brrrrrrap, tap, tap... tap, tap. The announcement man patted his wooden sticks against the small white drum hanging from his diminutive frame by a long fraying piece of blue ribbon. His bald head was visible through the ripped seam of his signature black top hat.

The man approached and circled the large crowd, continuing his inconsistent beat and increasing the villagers' suspense. Once he completed a full circle, he stopped, and the crowd parted to allow him entrance to the center.

As he passed Monique, she spied a playful smile pulling at the corner of his lips. Throughout the four years of daily announcements in the village, she had never seen the announcement man's grave expression altered, so she wondered what could possibly have affected his demeanor so profoundly.

He resumed the tap of his drumsticks on the tightly stretched silk. "Evening announcements for Friday, August 25th, 1944," he began. "Firstly, I want to inform you that a beloved member of our community, Pietro Beauvert, was murdered on the battlefield by our German enemies. Please keep Pietro and the Beauvert family in your prayers and add what you can spare to the donation box being prepared for them."

Murmurs echoed through the crowd as the villagers noticed the absence of Pietro's wife, Helene, and the Beauvert children. Everyone knew everyone in the small village.

"I think we should share some good news now, don't you agree?" the man continued, after a momentary pause of respect for the Beauvert family.

The villagers nodded, yearning for a distraction to their constant grief, but Anna fixed her gaze on the ground, her throat thickening as she thought of Emanuel.

Seeing her grandmother's body language, Monique sucked in her breath. She now regretted bringing her to the announcements. Instead of distracting Anna, Pietro's death had been another reminder of Emanuel's murder.

The man suddenly revealed his yellow teeth as a grin spread across his wrinkled cheeks. "Countrymen, the Allies have won! France has been liberated!"

Monique began pumping Anna's frail arm. "Omi! Did you hear him?"

Anna slowly lifted her gaze as the crowd erupted. Seemingly weightless, she was jostled back and forth by the villagers celebrating around her. She could not speak, nor did she dare even breathe.

"Omi!" Monique squealed, spinning her grandmother in a circle. "France is free! We are free!"

Anna's dull eyes became clouded with tears, and the chill that had overwhelmed her small body years ago began to ebb. She had lost so much, but she and Monique had somehow made it through. They could finally stop running for shelter.

Farmers threw their caps into the air, children were lifted onto their parents shoulders, and families danced in the streets. The cheers of the villagers bellowed through Buxières-les-Mines, and shortly after, someone reached the cathedral bell tower to begin the ringing of the bells that continued long into the night.

31 NOVEMBER 3RD, 1944

BUXIÈRES-LES-MINES, FRANCE

Liberation did not relieve Monique's arduous daily routine on the farm. Although Parisians were already experiencing increases in rations, the scarcity of food in the rural areas of France remained. Monique had learned from the announcement man that during the occupation, the French Resistance flooded the country with forged ration cards to overwhelm the German administration, so a completely new rationing system had been introduced by the provisional government, and its effects were only slowly trickling into the countryside. Daily chores still needed to be completed if Monique was going to earn enough to keep their room and board. The only difference for her was that she could imagine a day when her toil might end.

One evening, as the pink sun was dipping low on the Western horizon, Monique removed their single remaining turnip from the cupboard with dread, knowing that she would have to beg Nathan for something the following day. As she began dicing the lone vegetable, a knock on the room's door startled her. She wondered if Nathan had somehow felt her desperation.

She swung open the creaking door, squinting into the setting sun at a petite feminine form.

Monique's heart leapt. *Could it be? Could it finally be her mother?*

"Good afternoon, I'm looking for Inge Eisinger," said the female voice.

It was not Stella's.

"Sorry to disturb you," the woman continued as she shifted a stack of manilla folders from one arm to the other. "I'm Claudette Richard, a social worker. I was sent here by Ludwig Eisinger."

Monique's green eyes widened. It had been six years since that dreadful night in the apartment when she had last seen her father begging for his life, and she had tried to forget it ever since. A tight knot of cautious excitement coiled in Monique's stomach. Her father was alive, somehow. He had found her. And if he could find her, maybe Stella could too.

Monique blinked into the sunset. "Sorry, please, come in. It is a pleasure to meet you, Mademoiselle Richard. I'm Inge, Ludwig's daughter, but I go by Monique now." She shook Claudette's hand then gestured for her to sit down at the small table. "How did you find me?"

"It's a good story, but I would love to share it with you *and* your guardian," said the social worker, eyeing their sparse accommodations with pursed lips.

Monique hesitated. "My grandmother has been sick recently, so I'm not sure if she will wake up, but I can try."

She moved to the bed. "Omi, we have a visitor," she coaxed, lightly stroking Anna's thin gray hair. Monique silently pleaded with Anna to get up, concerned with both her lethargy and the fact that the social worker might take her away.

Claudette Richard rose from her chair as Anna stirred and gradually pushed herself up from the bed.

"Hello, it's nice to meet you," said Claudette. "I am a social worker. I was sent by Ludwig Eisinger."

Sensing the tension in the room and the importance of the situation, Anna reached for her cane. "Please excuse me," she whispered. "I have not been in good health recently. I am Monique's grandmother, Anna." She grasped the cane's head and pushed herself onto her feet. Monique helped her to the table.

"May I ask how you found us?" Anna inquired.

"Yes, of course," Claudette began as she rummaged through her folders. "A few months ago, Ludwig put an ad in *Aufbau*, a newspaper that helps people locate family members they were separated from during the war."

Monique sat quietly, processing the fact that her father had taken the initiative to find her, and her thoughts returned to the past.

"Papa? Papa? Where are you?" I yell over the din of the rowdy soccer stadium. I turn my head left and right, searching the concession tent in front of the outbuildings, but do not recognize his tall frame and green felt hat. Why do all of these men look the same? Where could he have gone? He was supposed to be waiting for me right here when I finished using the bathroom. Why did he leave?

I wander a few meters down the corridor toward the entrance to the stadium seats, but I still do not see him. Should I go back there? Is that where he went? Why didn't he wait for me? Entering the open air of the stadium, I peek up toward the direction of our seats, but I cannot remember exactly which are ours.

"Papa? Ludwig? Ludwig Eisinger?" I call out.

Suddenly, the stadium erupts around me. SK Rapid Wien has scored a goal in the final minutes of play, and everyone is on their feet, yelling and cheering. I can't even see the field with the number of bodies jumping up and down in front of me, how will I ever find him now?

I run back out toward the concession tent, tears filling my eyes. I don't know what to do. I am lost and alone, and I have no one to help me. Why did he leave me here alone?

"Inge! Inge!"

I turn toward the sound of my name. "Papa?"

"I'm here, Inge," says my father. "What's wrong? Why are you crying? I ran back into the stadium to watch the last few minutes of the game while you were busy out here. Then, when I returned, you were gone. Why did you leave this area without me?"

I turn my head away so that he cannot see my hot tears. He cares more about this soccer match than he does for me. I don't even know why he took me with him, since he is more interested in who wins the championship than spending time with his own daughter.

Monique had multiple memories of her father's absence. Even when she was a young child, he had never been interested in their relationship, abruptly entering and then disappearing from her life for years at a time. It stunned her that he would be interested in finding her now.

Anna listened stoically to Claudette's story. Monique glanced at her, wondering if her grandmother was concealing her fear of being separated from her, or if she had drifted off into the quiet, internal place she frequently escaped to.

Clearing her throat, the social worker paused and pasted on a smile to mask her officious tone. "Ludwig has requested that we move you to Clermont-Ferrand, here in France."

Monique's mouth set in a tight line, and the knot in her stomach clenched. He *did* want to take her away. How could he not have considered her grandmother? He knew how close they were. Even as a young child, Monique had spent every weekend with Anna. Her father was selfish, she decided, just like her mother had always said. She could never leave Anna, especially not now that she needed her help more than ever.

"Can my grandmother come?" Monique blurted out.

"Of course," Claudette chuckled. "Our goal is to reunite families, not split them apart. You and your grandmother will be moving together, and my organization will assist you financially."

Monique released her breath. Looking into Anna's usually absent eyes, she saw them wet with joy and relief.

"Thank you so much, Mademoiselle Richard," Monique gushed as she hugged the social worker. She knew that this move would save them from the endless cycle of poverty.

32 NOVEMBER 13TH, 1946

PARIS, FRANCE

It had been three months since Monique left Clermont-Ferrand, and two years since the awkward, stilted reunion with her father. As their relationship dissolved, she forged new ties with many of her neighbors, the Einstein family in particular. After their relocation, Anna's body was wracked by pneumonia, and she was hospitalized for a month. Rather than stay with her father, Monique accepted the Einstein's offer to stay with them. Their twin sons, who were six years older than Monique, began to view her like a sister.

Although she knew she would miss the Einsteins, Clermont-Ferrand had grown small around her. She yearned to feel the vitality of a metropolis once again, and decided it was time to make a move for herself for the first time in her life.

When Monique and Anna arrived in Paris, she could afford only meager accommodations on her new administrative salary. Their 100-square-foot rented room in the 10th Arrondissement reminded her of her time living with Emanuel, with one room tripling as a bedroom, kitchen, and living room. However, Monique was satisfied with her choice to leave Clermont-Ferrand. She enjoyed the endless energy of Paris and its inhabitants.

One evening, bundled up in the cobalt jacket that her mother had sent before the end of the war, Monique returned home late from work.

"Good evening," called Madame Martin, her neighbor, from the front walkway. Her face was buried into the collar of her coat to guard against the sharp cold.

"Nice to see you," Monique returned. She hurried up the steps and pulled open the reluctant door of their hotel. Before trudging up the stairs to the fourth floor, she retrieved the mail from the small room in the basement, sending cockroaches scurrying lower into the depths of the dank cellar.

A fresh pile of mail lay in the box, yet the envelopes were yellowed and rumpled, more uncollected posts from the war. Hoping for their passports, Monique searched the pile for something that read *Inge Eisinger* (she had not legally changed her name to Monique) *and Anna Kupfer*. But there were only solicitations.

Dispirited, Monique climbed the five sets of stairs to the top floor of the building. She opened the door to apartment 12A and called out, "Omi, I'm home."

Anna remained in the same position where Monique had left her at 6 a.m.: resting in the single bed with her eyes closed and gray hair spilling across the pillow.

"How are you feeling today, my Omi?" she asked, kneeling down and rousing her grandmother.

"Tired, my dear," croaked Anna, struggling to sit up. With trembling hands, she grasped the glass on the bedside table and took a long drink of water, then, licking her chapped lips, steadied her watery eyes on her granddaughter. Monique looked so beautiful and so mature—and so incredibly tired. Anna felt guilty for not working or helping with meals, for forcing her granddaughter to grow up so quickly.

"How was your day, my Monique?"

"It was great, Omi. Lie back down. I'm so sorry I'm late, but Monsieur Lamont needed me to finish a dictation. If I show him how much help I can be, he might offer me a full-time position in the administrative pool." Monique stood up. "Don't worry, supper will be ready soon."

Anna always knew when her granddaughter was lying to her, and it happened more often these days. Monique came home each evening looking discouraged and disheartened, and Anna wondered what aspect of her job caused this stress. Monique's boss seemed kind and supportive, though he did expect her to work long after the dinner hour. Defeated, Anna sank back onto the pillow.

Anna had already closed her eyes again as Monique reflected on the truth of her day. How had her day been? She sighed. It had been the same as every other day. She never concerned her grandmother with the frustration and boredom that plagued her working as a secretary, spending the day staring with envy and longing at the diplomas hanging on Monsieur Lamont's office walls. *If only I could save enough money to return to school*, she thought with sorrow.

Walking toward their alcohol burner, she reflected on the two lines of dialogue that she had managed to engage Anna in that night. It was one more than yesterday! She repeated this happy thought in her head, focusing on the small victory.

While the beans heated on the burner, Monique perused a magazine. The pages were filled with images of brightly clothed women, their carefree smiles allowing her to escape her reality if only for a short time. On the final page of the magazine, in an ad for the Red Cross, several children sat around a matronly teacher. *They must be orphans*, she thought, and hoped that they could be saved as Claudette Richard had saved her. Monique's heart began to ache. She wanted to be the woman in that picture. She wanted to help people, to be more than just a secretary. Ever since Claudette had freed them from their poverty in Buxières-les-Mines, Monique knew that she too wanted to become a social worker, to bring joy to those in need just as Claudette had for them. She would somehow get the schooling to become one, some day.

Monique put the magazine back down and noticed a small lilac-covered envelope on the table. Madame Martin must have dropped it off while checking in on Anna earlier. Her heart fluttered as she recognized the script on the envelope. This letter was from her mother.

Dozens of scenarios rushed through her mind as she snatched it up. Was she writing to tell them that she was moving back to Paris? Had she sent visas? Or had something happened to her? Monique began to read:

My dearest Inge,

I hope you and your Omi are staying warm and well. I recently moved to New York City alongside your new stepfather, Gerard Spitzer. Although very successful in Europe, my Gerard has struggled to get a job here in the United States. However, we have found a perfect apartment for two here in New York. I do hope that your Omi's health has improved. Please write back to me with any updates. It is my wish to see you both again soon. I miss you dearly.

All my love, Mutti

The letter burned in Monique's hand. It stung her that Stella was happily starting a new life without her in it and that she still failed to acknowledge her by her new name. Her dreams of reuniting with her mother in America were once again consumed by the shadows of her reality. To her mother, Monique realized, she would always just be in the background.

She tore the letter in half and threw it into the trash. Refusing to spend any more of them on her mother, she blinked her tears away—and noticed a second envelope on the table. Her fingers traced the edges of the stamp marked with a soaring eagle. "U.S. Citizenship and Immigration Services," she read.

"Omi, wake up!" she exclaimed, running to the bed and nudging her shoulder.

"What is it, Monique?" gasped Anna.

"I think this is it!" she yelled. Heart racing, she ripped open the envelope, and two green papers fell onto the bed. "It's the visas, Omi. They're here! They are finally here!"

33 DECEMBER 10TH, 1946

ATLANTIC OCEAN

The *Île-de-France* exhaled loudly as Monique emerged onto the top deck. Regal women stood at the railings wearing dark furs and headscarves that danced in the light breeze while well-dressed men shielded them from the spray of the sea. She found an empty spot on the railing and leaned out over the barrier as far as she could to take in the ocean. The sharp, cold air slapped her cheeks, and her fiery hair flew around her head as if angered by the elements. There were no ships for as far as she could see, and the calm, undisturbed water made her feel at peace. On the horizon, only a few flat clouds designated the change between the sky and the sea.

The depthless water seemed as empty as her heart during the past eight years. She had suffered such longing for the security and stability that her mother once offered, but now, she wondered if it would ever be given to her again—or if she would even accept it. Stella had left her alone and unprotected, exposed and vulnerable to the inhumanities of war, so Monique had become her own shield, guarding against the threat of homelessness and hunger. She had grown accustomed to the weight of the responsibility, for her grandmother and for herself.

When their last afternoon in Paris had arrived, Monique had busied herself collecting her few belongings into the same bag that she had first carried as she left Austria eight years before. Throughout her lonely journey, she had carried that bag forward with dread, never certain of her destination and the new terrors she might find there. As she boarded the ship two weeks ago, however, she was not afraid. She strode boldly into the future, swinging her bag with excitement, ready to take on the new world.

"Omi, a few minutes ago, the first mate reported that we will be arriving in New York City very soon!" Monique announced to Anna as she entered their tiny stateroom.

Anna nodded weakly.

"I want to go back out to the deck and watch our arrival. Won't you come with me, Omi?" Monique asked.

Anna said nothing in an attempt to mask her emotion; she knew she would not be able to control her voice. Where she truly wanted to be going was Vienna. She loved her home with the same ferocity that she loved her granddaughter, and she thought it a cruelty that she had been forced to choose between them. It had taken all of her will to pack up the few belongings that remained on their final morning in Paris, understanding that she would never return to her beloved European homeland. The last item, Emanuel's navy cardigan sweater, she had held against her face, breathing in its scent and hiding her tears. Then, resolved, she had folded it carefully and placed it in the bag.

As they had walked to the train station, Anna leaned almost entirely on Monique, not due to her physical ailments so much as her intense sorrow.

"Please, please Omi?" Monique pressed, and Anna allowed herself to be led from the room.

They entered the open area of the lower deck and joined the

other third-class families scattered along the railing. Monique wrinkled her nose as she breathed in the odor of oil and sewage, realizing that the ocean was behind them. They were approaching the Upper Bay, so Monique placed one of Anna's hands onto an empty spot on the cold metal railing to steady her. She feared the waterway would become choppy.

"I think that is Manhattan Island!" exclaimed a man, pointing to the tall dark shadows rising from the fringes of their vision, and his children began to cheer and jump up and down. Monique had to consciously remind herself of her age to stop from joining them.

"We're almost there," she whispered into Anna's ear, giving her a tight hug, and she saw her grandmother smile for the first time in many months.

When the color of the water had completely lost its clarity, turning into a brown, muddied color, Monique knew that they had entered the Hudson River. She squinted into the horizon and searched the eastern landscape for a glimpse of America's Lady Liberty, their symbol of freedom. The statue's blurry greenish hue began to materialize, and shortly, Monique could make out the points of her crown and the folds of her robe. Stretching her chin up as high as she could to catch sight of the torch, a beacon to the lost and wandering, Monique felt light-headed. She had waited for nearly a decade to be rescued from the nightmares of the war. Overcoming displacement, violence, starvation, and extreme loneliness, she was finally being guided into safe harbor.

The *Île-de-France* blew its horn, announcing their arrival into New York, just as it slipped into the shadow of Lady Liberty. The statue dwarfed the ship, eclipsing the passengers with her magnitude and grace, comforting them with a sense of security and protection.

Ignoring the screams of delight from the children around her, Monique turned to focus on Anna's strong face. Her grandmother had been her protector and guardian for all of those long years in peril. She wrapped her arms around Anna. "Omi," she breathed, her voice heavy with emotion. "Omi, we made it."

Anna's eyes sparkled, a glimmer of hope illuminating them. She leaned onto Monique and used the breath she had been saving to speak to Monique. "My darling, you are so strong and brave. I am in awe of your courage. You do not need to continue running for shelter anymore. Your life without shelter begins today." Anna paused. "I have protected you from some very important information about our family so that you would be safe, but it is time for you to know the truth."

Monique held her breath as Anna spoke, "Monique, you are Jewish."

34 EPILOGUE WRITTEN BY MONIQUE (INGE) SHEFT

JULY 2021

For many years, I buried my past. It was partially because I wanted to shelter my children from this part of my life, but also because I believed no one was really interested in it. However, my son, Peter, became very interested in all the details and background of my childhood as he began to research that period of history and look into my past.

Currently, my granddaughter, Suzette, is the reason I think about my past more often. When I reflect on my experience during a war that began 81 years ago, I immediately think about the deep loneliness and fear I felt. I spent my teenage years and childhood without my mother, who left for America, and my uncle, who died in combat. My only family member was my Omi who was quite ill. My sorrow only escalated when my best friend, Jacqueline, was killed by a bomb. These events ensured that survival was my principal goal. I used to daydream and invent scenarios about when I would see my mother again, which gave me hope for a future.

The fear I felt during the war was deep-seated. I feared my Omi's condition deteriorating, not finding our next meal, and the chance of a bomb or an attack. I felt deeply grateful when the Americans came to our aid and the celebration of the villagers when we were liberated. I will forever be extremely appreciative to the soldiers who lost their lives fighting to free us—they are the reason we are alive today.

However, when I arrived in America, I was lonely once again. No one in America shared my experience of the war; their country remained untouched by its horrors. I found it hurtful that the Americans were oblivious to the human suffering the soldiers had witnessed, so in my adult life, I paid my respects to these courageous soldiers by visiting the beaches of Normandy. I was absolutely amazed by how they were able to land on such deep rocks in such horrendous weather conditions. I felt such sorrow at the cemetery where I saw the names of so many brave young souls who were mostly around 20 and 21 when they died. I felt extremely blessed to have been able to forge a family of my own, as I never had that before. Moreover, my starvation and poverty during the war are the reason I desire to help those in need, like hungry, afraid, underprivileged children.

My wish is that no child should ever experience such horrors again, so in order to prevent the recurrence of an event like the Holocaust, I hope that schools will educate children about it in order to help terminate prejudices in America.

When I arrived in America in 1946, I was extremely fortunate to be blissfully unaware of antisemitism; I was too preoccupied with learning English, attending high school, and adjusting to life in a new country. However, now I see racism against minorities, as well as antisemitism and Islamophobia. I hope that we have not overcome the Holocaust only for new prejudices and divisions to occur in the world. Therefore, I hope we can become a united people where all are accepted, no matter their religion or race. Lastly, I am unbelievably proud of Suzette for educating others on our history.

ACKNOWLEDGMENTS

There are so many people without whom this story would not exist. Thank you to each and every one of you who inspired and guided me throughout this process.

I want to begin by thanking my dad, Peter, whose passion for history, Judaism, and our family heritage inspired me to write and finish this book. I also want to thank my mom, Nancy, who has taught me to chase after my passions and never stop writing. Without your encouraging words and guidance I know this book would have been unachievable. Finally, I want to thank my brother, Grant, who believed in me. I love you all so much.

Another thank you to so many people who have been incredibly helpful in many different ways: Brian Marcus, Brooke Fichera, Chris Ajemian, Iain Barr, Leah Paulos, Luisa Colón, and Megan Campbell Reigner. I cannot thank all of you enough for your support throughout this process.

I would also like to thank the USC Shoah Foundation for recording my grandmother's story, and that of so many others; the details in your recording have grounded many of the stories in my book.

Thank you so much to my publisher, Liesbeth Heenk, who took a risk by working with a teenage author and provided me with a once in a lifetime opportunity. I will forever be grateful that you trusted and believed in me.

And most importantly, I want to give my Omi, Monique (Inge), a huge thank you. I feel so immensely grateful that you trusted me to record your story and that you gave me an opportunity to bring it to life again through writing. I will always be indebted to you for the kindness, willingness, and support you showed me throughout this process. I love you so much.

PHOTOS

View of St. Stephen's Cathedral from Inge's window, Vienna, Austria

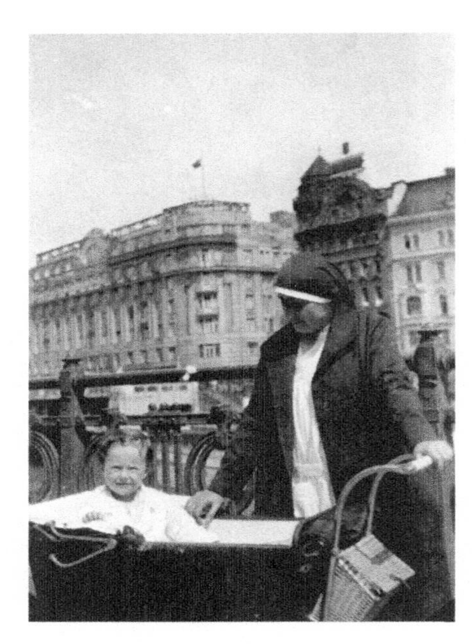

Inge with her baby nurse, Vienna, Austria, 1931.

Inge with her mother, Stella Eisinger, Vienna, Austria.

Inge with her father, Ludwig Eisinger, Vienna, Austria.

Inge (left) and her host brother, Michel (right), Paris, 1939.

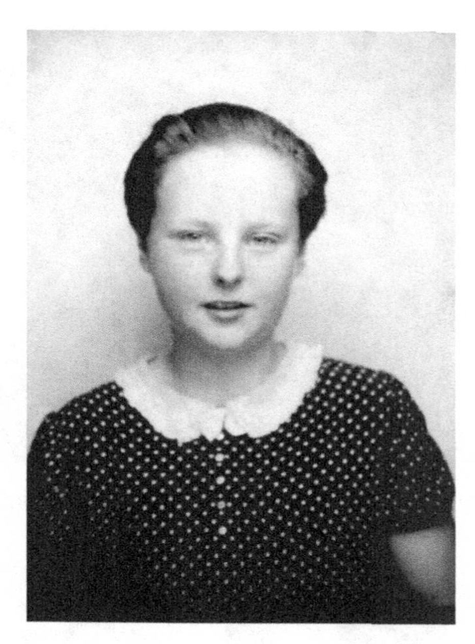

Inge at the boarding school in the outskirts of Paris.

Emanuel Kupfer in the French Foreign Legion,
December, 1940.

Emanuel with his French Foreign Legion troop, December, 1940.

Inge with other children, second from left.

Inge (front left) and friends in Buxières-les-Mines, France.

Inge with her grandmother, Anna Kupfer, in Buxières-les-Mines, France, 1941.

Inge in Buxières-les-Mines, France, 1942.

Inge, circa 1946.

Inge, circa 1946.

Inge, circa 1946.

Anna, circa 1946.

ABOUT THE AUTHOR

Suzette Sheft (2006) attends the Horace Mann School in New York City. She lives in Manhattan with her mother, twin brother, and two dogs. In her free time, she enjoys writing, reading, running, and spending time with family and friends.

She began writing *Running for Shelter* at age 13 and recently earned a Silver Key from Scholastic for an excerpt of the book. Suzette hopes that her novel inspires other children to record important stories from their own family legacies.

AMSTERDAM PUBLISHERS HOLOCAUST LIBRARY

The series **Holocaust Survivor Memoirs World War II** consists of the following autobiographies of survivors:

Outcry. Holocaust Memoirs, by Manny Steinberg

Hank Brodt Holocaust Memoirs. A Candle and a Promise, by Deborah Donnelly

The Dead Years. Holocaust Memoirs, by Joseph Schupack

Rescued from the Ashes. The Diary of Leokadia Schmidt, Survivor of the Warsaw Ghetto, by Leokadia Schmidt

My Lvov. Holocaust Memoir of a twelve-year-old Girl, by Janina Hescheles

Remembering Ravensbrück. From Holocaust to Healing, by Natalie Hess

Wolf. A Story of Hate, by Zeev Scheinwald with Ella Scheinwald

Save my Children. An Astonishing Tale of Survival and its Unlikely Hero, by Leon Kleiner with Edwin Stepp

Holocaust Memoirs of a Bergen-Belsen Survivor & Classmate of Anne Frank, by Nanette Blitz Konig

Defiant German - Defiant Jew. A Holocaust Memoir from inside the Third Reich, by Walter Leopold with Les Leopold

In a Land of Forest and Darkness. The Holocaust Story of two Jewish Partisans, by Sara Lustigman Omelinski

Holocaust Memories. Annihilation and Survival in Slovakia, by Paul Davidovits

From Auschwitz with Love. The Inspiring Memoir of Two Sisters' Survival, Devotion and Triumph Told by Manci Grunberger Beran & Ruth Grunberger Mermelstein, by Daniel Seymour

Remetz. Resistance Fighter and Survivor of the Warsaw Ghetto, by Jan Yohay Remetz

My March Through Hell. A Young Girl's Terrifying Journey to Survival, by Halina Kleiner with Edwin Stepp

---

The series **Holocaust Survivor True Stories WWII** consists of the following biographies:

Among the Reeds. The true story of how a family survived the Holocaust, by Tammy Bottner

A Holocaust Memoir of Love & Resilience. Mama's Survival from Lithuania to America, by Ettie Zilber

Living among the Dead. My Grandmother's Holocaust Survival Story of Love and Strength, by Adena Bernstein Astrowsky

Heart Songs. A Holocaust Memoir, by Barbara Gilford

Shoes of the Shoah. The Tomorrow of Yesterday, by Dorothy Pierce

Hidden in Berlin. A Holocaust Memoir, by Evelyn Joseph Grossman

Separated Together. The Incredible True WWII Story of Soulmates Stranded an Ocean Apart, by Kenneth P. Price, Ph.D.

The Man Across the River. The incredible story of one man's will to survive the Holocaust, by Zvi Wiesenfeld

If Anyone Calls, Tell Them I Died. A Memoir, by Emanuel (Manu) Rosen

The House on Thrömerstrasse. A Story of Rebirth and Renewal in the Wake of the Holocaust, by Ron Vincent

Dancing with my Father. His hidden past. Her quest for truth. How Nazi Vienna shaped a family's identity, by Jo Sorochinsky

The Story Keeper. Weaving the Threads of Time and Memory - A Memoir, by Fred Feldman

Krisia's Silence. The Girl who was not on Schindler's List, by Ronny Hein

Defying Death on the Danube. A Holocaust Survival Story, by Debbie J. Callahan with Henry Stern

A Doorway to Heroism. A decorated German-Jewish Soldier who became an American Hero, by Rabbi W. Jack Romberg

The Shoemaker's Son. The Life of a Holocaust Resister, by Laura Beth Bakst

The Redhead of Auschwitz. A True Story, by Nechama Birnbaum

Land of Many Bridges. My Father's Story, by Bela Ruth Samuel Tenenholtz

Creating Beauty from the Abyss. The Amazing Story of Sam Herciger, Auschwitz Survivor and Artist, by Lesley Ann Richardson

On Sunny Days We Sang. A Holocaust Story of Survival and Resilience, by Jeannette Grunhaus de Gelman

Painful Joy. A Holocaust Family Memoir, by Max J. Friedman

I Give You My Heart. A True Story of Courage and Survival, by Wendy Holden

In the Time of Madmen, by Mark A. Prelas

Monsters and Miracles. Horror, Heroes and the Holocaust, by Ira Wesley Kitmacher

Flower of Vlora. Growing up Jewish in Communist Albania, by Anna Kohen

Aftermath: Coming of Age on Three Continents. A Memoir, by Annette Libeskind Berkovits

Not a real Enemy. The True Story of a Hungarian Jewish Man's Fight for Freedom, by Robert Wolf

Zaidy's War. Four Armies, Three Continents, Two Brothers. One Man's Impossible Story of Endurance, by Martin Bodek

The Glassmaker's Son. Looking for the World my Father left behind in Nazi Germany, by Peter Kupfer

The Apprentice of Buchenwald. The True Story of the Teenage Boy Who Sabotaged Hitler's War Machine, by Oren Schneider

The Cello Still Sings. A Generational Story of the Holocaust and of the Transformative Power of Music, by Janet Horvath

---

The series **Jewish Children in the Holocaust** consists of the following autobiographies of Jewish children hidden during WWII in the Netherlands:

Searching for Home. The Impact of WWII on a Hidden Child, by Joseph Gosler

See You Tonight and Promise to be a Good Boy! War memories, by Salo Muller

Sounds from Silence. Reflections of a Child Holocaust Survivor, Psychiatrist and Teacher, by Robert Krell

Sabine's Odyssey. A Hidden Child and her Dutch Rescuers, by Agnes Schipper

The Journey of a Hidden Child, by Harry Pila with Robin Black

---

The series **New Jewish Fiction** consists of the following novels, written by Jewish authors. All novels are set in the time during or after the Holocaust.

The Corset Maker. A Novel, by Annette Libeskind Berkovits

Escaping the Whale. The Holocaust is over. But is it ever over for the next generation? by Ruth Rotkowitz

When the Music Stopped. Willy Rosen's Holocaust, by Casey Hayes

Hands of Gold. One Man's Quest to Find the Silver Lining in Misfortune, by Roni Robbins

The Girl Who Counted Numbers. A Novel, by Roslyn Bernstein

There was a garden in Nuremberg. A Novel, by Navina Michal Clemerson

The Butterfly and the Axe, by Omer Bartov

Good for a Single Journey, by Helen Joyce

The series **Holocaust Books for Young Adults** consists of the following novels, based on true stories:

The Boy behind the Door. How Salomon Kool Escaped the Nazis. Inspired by a True Story, by David Tabatsky

Running for Shelter. A True Story, by Suzette Sheft

The Precious Few. An Inspirational Saga of Courage based on True Stories, by David Twain with Art Twain

Jacob's Courage: A Holocaust Love Story, by Charles S. Weinblatt

---

The series **WW2 Historical Fiction** consists of the following novels, some of which are based on true stories:

Mendelevski's Box. A Heartwarming and Heartbreaking Jewish Survivor's Story, by Roger Swindells

A Quiet Genocide. The Untold Holocaust of Disabled Children WW2 Germany, by Glenn Bryant

The Knife-Edge Path, by Patrick T. Leahy

Brave Face. The Inspiring WWII Memoir of a Dutch/German Child, by I. Caroline Crocker and Meta A. Evenly

When We Had Wings. The Gripping Story of an Orphan in Janusz Korczak's Orphanage. A Historical Novel, by Tami Shem-Tov

Want to be an AP book reviewer?

Reviews are very important in a world dominated by the social media and social proof. Please drop us a line if you want to join the *AP review team.* We will then add you to our list of advance reviewers. No strings attached, and we promise that we will not be spamming you.

info@amsterdampublishers.com

Made in the USA
Las Vegas, NV
11 March 2024